C000234950

St Pancras Station

First published by George Allen and Unwin Ltd in 1968
Republished by Historical Publications 2003,
revised and with a new final chapter by Robert Thorne.

© **Jack Simmons 1968**
© **For the chapter entitled 'St Pancras Revived', RobertThorne 2003**

ISBN 0 948667 68 0

The moral right of the authors has been asserted
All rights reserved; unauthorised duplication contravenes applicable laws

Typeset by Historical Publications Ltd
Reproduction by Square Group, SE1
Printing by Edelvives, Zaragoza, Spain

ST PANCRAS STATION

by Jack Simmons
revised and with a new chapter by
Robert Thorne

It is impossible to regard the vast buildings and their dependencies, which constitute a chief terminal station of a great line of railway, without feelings of inexpressible astonishment at the magnitude of the capital and the boldness of the enterprise, which are manifested in the operations of which they are the stage.

Nothing in the history of the past affords any parallel to such a spectacle.

DIONYSIUS LARDNER, *Railway Economy* (1850)

HISTORICAL PUBLICATIONS

TO DAVID TREFFREY

Contents

Colour plates are between pages 80 and 89

List of Illustrations

LIST OF ILLUSTRATIONS

Abbreviations

Barnes   E G Barnes, *The Rise of the Midland Railway, 1844-74* (1966).

M.P.I.C.E.   *Minutes of Proceedings of the Institution of Civil Engineers.*

P.P.   *Parliamentary Papers.* The references are to the continuosly-paginated volumes of the set in the British Library.

P.R.O.   Public Record Office.

Williams   F S Williams, *The Midland Railway* (1876).

Jack Simmons 1915-2000

Jack Simmons transformed the study of British railway history by applying to it the standards of the best academic history – meticulous accuracy, a disciplined curiosity and clear, economic prose. He was interested in railways from boyhood, not just as someone who loved to travel by train but as a topographer fascinated by English towns and countryside and the impact which railways had upon them. He was also drawn to the subject by an admiration for the Victorians, above all their energy, seriousness, sense of duty and attention to detail, qualities apparent in all the great railway promoters and managers.

He was not always known as a railway historian. His first reputation was as a historian of imperialism, especially colonial Africa. With Margery Perham he edited *African Discovery: An Anthology of Exploration* (1942) and he published a succinct biography of David Livingstone (*Livingstone and Africa*, 1955). But as well as the grand theme of Britain's role overseas he was equally committed to the local history of counties, towns and parishes. Following his appointment as the first Professor of History at the University of Leicester, he promoted a variety of historical sub-disciplines, particularly local history, and he showed the relevance of this approach in his work on counties such as Devon and Leicestershire. He was a key figure in the development of the university until his retirement in 1975.

The railway theme began to emerge more prominently in his publications in the 1960s, particularly his brilliant summary, *The Railways of Britain. An Historical Introduction* (1961). After his retirement he poured his knowledge into a series of books on the vintage years of railway development, including *The Railway in Town and Country 1830 – 1914* (1986) and *The Victorian Railway* (1991), and finally into editing with Gordon Biddle, *The Oxford Companion to British Railway History* (1997).

Long before it became fashionable, Jack Simmons urged historians to use artefacts and the landscape as evidence of the past, alongside books and documents. For railways that meant the physical evidence of locomotives, equipment, track and above all buildings. This book on St. Pancras Station, first published in 1968, epitomised what he urged others to do because in it he sought to combine political, technical, architectural and social history. By focusing on a single building, one which he cared about passionately, he demonstrated more clearly than in any of his other books how relevant and engaging railway history could be.

Preface
to the first edition

This book has grown out of a lecture given in the University of Leicester in December, 1965. It figured there as the last of a series on 'Seven Great Monuments'. At the end of the lecture, though at that time no public announcement had been made of an intention to shut the station down, I told my audience that I thought this might well be proposed before long. The proposal came little more than six months later. The argument it gave rise to is set out below *(pp. 138-143)*. The future of the building is still doubtful, but its ultimate preservation now seems more likely than at any time since the argument began.

The purpose of this study is to descibe the history of the building in relation to the functions it was designed to perform. Such studies of buildings of the nineteenth century have been, in my opinion, too rare. We have not had one, for example, for any of the great London hotels, museums, or banks. St Pancras was, and is, a railway buidling; the operation of trains into and out of the station, the kind of service they provided for passengers – these form an important part of my story. My subject is the passenger station and the hotel that was, from the outset, conceived as an integral part of it. But I have, I hope, said just enough of the adjacent goods stations and of the St Pancras Branch, which burrows beneath the main station to join the Metropolitan line underground, to furnish the reader with an account of the whole of the complex installation developed by the Midland Railway at St Pancras.

This is, then, a book concerned chiefly with transport. But I have also tried to explain what seem to me to be the issues involved in the long argument about the merits of St Pancras station as a building. I have treated it historically, and I hope my opinions will not be found intrusive. Let me make it clear at the outset that I admire it profoundly – both the logical exactitude of the train-shed and the rich exuberance of the hotel. Having said that, I try to tell a plain tale, made up of fact and of other people's opinions, with no more than a very occasional fleer at those I dislike, until Chapter VI, which is personal. Nobody need agree with me; but I hope that those who are concerned in the long controversy that lies ahead will pay attention to the remarkable history of the building, recognizing that, whether they themselves like it or not, it is one of the most perfect monuments of the life and thinking of the Victorian age.

The publishers and I are grateful to those who have supplied the illustrations that have been used; the sources of all of them are acknowledged in the List of Illustrations.

I have been generously helped by librarians and archivists: at the British Museum, the Royal Institute of British Architects, the Reference Library of the Borough of Camden, the Patent Office, the National Monuments Record and – most especially – the Historical Records Department of British Railways, where Mr Atkinson and his colleagues do so much for those who consult the magnificent series of records in their charge.

I am grateful to Mr J Barrow and Mr P C Jamieson, who kindly allowed me to read their unpublished theses on St Pancras station; to Professor P A W Coollins, who elucidated for me the authorship of the famous essay on Agar Town in *Household Words*; and to Dr J M Crook, who is well versed in the history of the Gothic Revival in the Victorian age. He read the text for me in draft, and his criticsm of my treatment of the architectural history of the building has greatly helped me to improve it.

JS
The University, Leicester
April 25, 1968

Preface to Second Edition

The publication of the first edition of this book in 1968 was occasioned by a crisis in the life of St. Pancras Station. As Jack Simmons said in his Preface to that edition, this is for the most part a dispassionate account of the building's history, but it is obvious almost from page one where his loyalties lay. He immensely admired the building and the people who brought it into existence, and the aphorisms and phrases which colour the text clearly fore-tell the substance of his concluding remarks. His decisiveness, plus his authoritative com-mand of the facts, gave the book its characteristic tone, and they played a significant part in securing the future of the building.

Although it served a particular purpose when it was first published, this book was always meant to be a permanent record of St. Pancras Station. True to that intent, it has been constantly in demand, amongst those who have an interest in the building and also amongst historians who regard it as a model study of its kind. This demand has of course considerably increased now that the project to bring the Channel Tunnel Rail Link to St. Pancras is being carried out.

Knowing that a new edition would be welcomed, Jack Simmons asked me whether I would help him revise and update the original text and add a chapter of my own describ-ing what has happened since 1968. We set out together on this project, but since his death in September 2000 I have had to carry on alone, unaided by the discernment that he brought to everything he did. Where his original text is concerned, I have done little more than to add new knowledge that has come to hand and amend passages where what he described no longer exists, or can no longer be referred to in the present tense. Hopefully these changes are not discordant or obtrusive. The additional chapter never had the benefit of his comments: he probably would have welcomed a few more jibes at politicians, but not at the expense of telling a clear story of events as they have unfolded. At a more mundane level, he insisted that we update the footnotes, and that I have done.

In his original Preface Jack Simmons thanked the librarians and archivists of various libraries and institutions. Thirty-five years on, their successors have been just as help-ful, particularly the staff at the Public Record Office and the National Railway Museum at York. In addition I am indebted to all those with whom I have worked on the project to bring the Midland Grand Hotel to life again, in particular Stephen Jordan, Ray Willis, and Alastair Lansley at London and Continental Railways, Angus Boag of Manhattan Lofts, Hugh Davies of Whitbread Hotels, my colleagues at Alan Baxter & Associates especially William Filmer-Sankey, and Zoë Croad at English Heritage. Others have jumped into action when I have asked for help including Margaret Davies, Nick Derby-shire, Geoff Goslin, Malcolm Holmes, Randall Keynes, Keith Scholey, and above all my wife Liz Robinson. They may not like what I have written, but their corrections can be incorporated when the next edition comes along!

RT
London,
July 2003

CHAPTER I

The Midland Railway

ST PANCRAS station was the child of the Midland Railway. Its character, its form and scale, can be understood only in the light of the history of the company that built it.

The Midland Railway Company was created in 1844 by the amalgamation, under Act of Parliament, of three existing companies: the Midland Counties, the Birmingham & Derby Junction, and the North Midland.[1] Taken together, the lines of these companies formed one coherent system, 180 miles long, centred on Derby, where they all met. The new company had complete control of the traffic between Birmingham, Leicester, Nottingham, and Leeds; and it formed an important section of the earliest railway route from London to Scotland, by way of Rugby and York.

The first Chairman of the Midland Company was George Hudson. It became the strongest and most stable part of the railway empire he built up and reigned over during the next five years. When his power collapsed and his empire fell apart, the Midland held together under the prudent direction of John Ellis, emerging in the 'fifties, after much tribulation, as one of the soundest railway properties in the kingdom, with a dividend on its Ordinary shares rising from the wretched 2 per cent of the disastrous year 1850 to $3\frac{5}{8}$ per cent in 1854 and 1855. By 1852 its system comprised about 500 route miles (including lines worked, though not owned, by the Company), stretching from Bristol to Leeds and Morecambe, and to Lincoln and Peterborough in the east. The heart of it all remained at Derby. It was exactly what its title implied, a railway serving the Midlands.

But the very nature of its central position obliged it to be more than that. Its interests thrust out beyond Bristol into the West Country; it was already pushing up into the Peak District towards Manchester; at Lancaster and Normanton it exchanged traffic with other companies to and from Scotland; Peterborough was its gateway to East Anglia. Most notably, it lacked its own outlet to London. All London traffic from the Midland system had to pass through Rugby, and so up the London & North Western main line to Euston.

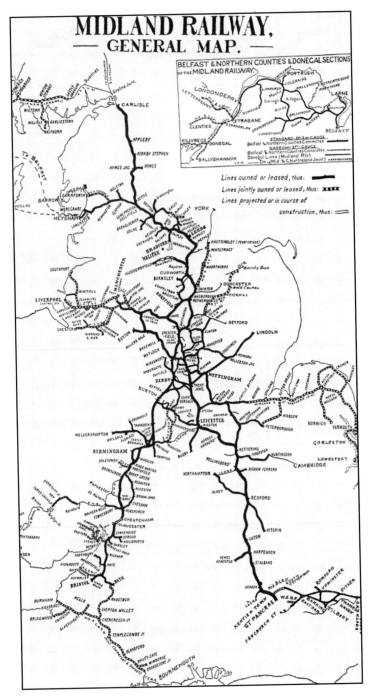

1. Map of the Midland Railway from the Railway Year Book *for 1914.*

The Company was tempted to extend its lines in all these directions; and eventually it did so, until by the end of the nineteenth century – either in its own right or through undertakings owned jointly with other companies – its tentacles reached out to Bournemouth, Swansea, Liverpool, Carlisle, and Yarmouth *(ill. 1)*. In the 1840s and 1850s this lay in the future. The two outward thrusts that most exercised the Company then were those to Manchester and London.

As far as Manchester was concerned, the work began with the construction of the line from Ambergate through Matlock to Rowsley, authorized in 1846 and opened three years afterwards. From 1853 onwards the Midland started to press further, against stiff opposition from rival companies, until it achieved its objective in 1867. This was a difficult and expensive operation, which involved the driving of a railway through the heart of the Peak District rising up to 1,000 feet above sea-level and piercing the hills with a dozen tunnels. The construction of an alternative line to London, though it would run through a much easier terrain, would be even more costly. It is not surprising that the Company hesitated a long time before committing itself to such an enterprise.

The first notion of it was started in 1845, in the merry days of the Railway Mania, when projectors were dazzled by visions of limitless capital, earning extravagant dividends. It was already a serious nuisance to the Midland Railway that its London traffic had to be handed over to another company at Rugby. There were inevitable delays in the transference of passengers and goods there; the line to Euston easily became congested – especially since in the forties the main motive power employed on it consisted of the very small engines designed by Edward Bury. Another great line was now planned from London to the North, the Great Northern. Though Hudson and the Midland Company had opposed it fiercely when it was before Parliament, once it had been authorized (in 1846) and moved towards reality they came to terms with it. One sign of that was their support for a railway from Leicester to Hitchin, where it would join the Great Northern – at a point only 32 miles from London, or 50 miles nearer than Rugby. The Bill for this line was approved by Parliament in July 1847, but by that time money for such projects was already becoming tight, and it was quietly abandoned in 1850.

The matter could not rest there, however. As the Midland Company's system grew, and especially as the coal from Yorkshire and the Midlands began to find its way by rail into the London market, the delays at Rugby and on the London & North Western line became more and more exasperating. Nor were the Midland's interests involved alone. The Leicester & Hitchin scheme had promised to open up to railways a large tract of Leicestershire, Northamptonshire, and Bedfordshire in which there were either no railways at all or railways running east and west, not southwards to London. The business men and landowners in this large district were not disposed to forgo the benefits that the Leicester & Hitchin line would have brought them. They were indignant that it had been abandoned, especially since the Midland Company had given an undertaking that it should be completed within two years of its authorization.

Early in 1852 a deputation of those who had been most closely concerned with the Leicester & Hitchin scheme went to Derby for an interview with the Directors of the Midland Company. Among its members was William Whitbread of Southill, who had been a consistent and urgent advocate of railways in Bedfordshire since 1845. He was the largest landowner in the county after the Duke of Bedford – it was computed, indeed, that an eighth of all the land that would be required for the railway from Leicester to Hitchin was in his possession. The Midland Directors were clearly impressed by the arguments advanced at the meeting, and especially by the very plain indication given to them by their visitors that if the Midland refused to sponsor the railway they wanted they would turn to the Great Northern – whose line was now almost complete from Yorkshire to King's Cross – instead. This was a serious threat to the Midland Company, in terms of railway strategy, for it would mean opening up Leicester and the South Midlands to a dangerous rival.

With such considerations in mind, the Midland Board decided to go ahead. It quickly established a Leicester & Hitchin Extension Committee, under whose instructions Charles Liddell undertook a fresh survey and recommended the adoption of a route from Wigston Magna through Market Harborough, Desborough, Kettering, and Bedford to a junction with the Great Northern just north of Hitchin. This plan passed through Parliament without difficulty in 1853.[2]

The building of the line proceeded slowly. It was due for completion in 1856, but was not in fact opened to all traffic until May 1857.[3]

The Midland Company now had its second means of access to London. It made full use of both routes for its steadily mounting business and pressed its partners for further improvements in them. The London & North Western Company built a third line, chiefly to accommodate the Midland freight traffic, almost the whole way from Bletchley to the tunnel under Primrose Hill in North London in 1859. The Midland secured running powers, for seven years in the first instance, over the Great Northern line south of Hitchin. In 1858 it began to work through trains into and out of King's Cross, and passengers were permitted to book from King's Cross to stations on the Midland system as freely as they had been able to do from Euston since 1840.[4] The Great Northern Company also agreed to allow the Midland to build a coal depot of its own to the west of King's Cross. This was a nicely-calculated decision, which may not have been to the advantage of the Great Northern.[5] It encouraged the Midland's exploitation of the immensely valuable coal trade to London, at a time when the Great Northern Company itself was experiencing great difficulty with rival railways and with the coal owners in South Yorkshire. The Midland was rapidly securing a firm grip on this business. It claimed to have been the first railway company to carry coal from inland pits to London; in 1862 it brought in 800,000 tons – nearly 18 per cent of the capital's total consumption.[6] The Midland agreed to pay the Great Northern a minimum toll of £20,000 a year for the exercise of its running powers, and this was a substantial addition to the income the Great Northern could derive from its own operations between Hitchin and London.

There was a still more powerful reason why the Great Northern was prepared to treat the Midland favourably. It was already being rumoured that the Midland was contemplating the construction of its own line to London. That would be detrimental to the interests of the Great Northern, which would both lose the income from tolls it was enjoying and see its chief competitor advantageously established in the capital, in complete independence. From its point of view there was much to be said for trying to keep things as they were, even if that meant sacrifices and further concessions to the Midland.

The position changed, however, in 1862. As soon as it was decided, early in 1860, that a second International Exhibition was to be held in London two years hence,[7] the managers of the railway companies serving London began to prepare for a rush of ordinary and excursion traffic even more formidable than that of 1851. The line from Hitchin to King's Cross was already occupied for much of the day, as intensively as current methods of operation, with an imperfect block system, allowed. It was clear, before the Exhibition opened, that the Great Northern line would be quite unable to cope with the traffic that would be placed upon it that summer. King's Cross station itself, as might have been expected, quickly became grossly overcrowded, and there were loud complaints at the annoyances that passengers suffered.[8] On June 20th, less than three weeks after the Exhibition began, the Great Northern felt it necessary to require that its sidings at King's Cross should be vacated by the Midland trains that had previously been accommodated there, justifying this step by pointing out that the new Midland coal station was nearly complete and could afford these facilities instead. When the Midland delayed in meeting this demand, the Great Northern evicted two of its coal trains and subjected Midland passengers to systematically increasing discomfort.

Both the warring parties deserve our sympathy. The Midland's demands were legitimate, and it was powerless to control the situation. The Great Northern felt pressed to death, obliged to take a step that was contrary to many of its own best interests. The events of June and July 1862 made it plain that only one solution was possible in the long run: that the Midland should withdraw from its tenancy, carrying its traffic to London by a line of its own.

In the past it has usually bee supposed that these events were the cause of the Midland Company's decision to promote a London extension; and it is certainly true that, after somewhat unrealistic negotiations had been tried with the Great Northern, the Midland Board formally decided to institute a survey for a line from Bedford to London on October 14th of this same year. But Mr Barnes has pointed out that in the previous December the Midland Company had been buying land in the parish of St Pancras, much in excess of what it needed for its new goods station.[9] It is clear that the management had already decided, before the summer crisis, that the new line would have to be built. The question was not 'whether?', only 'when?'[10]

*   *   *   *

Let us now turn to look a little more closely at the Company and at the men who were directing it in 1862. Its prosperity was established for all to see: with a paid-up capital of some £18 million, yielding a dividend on its Ordinary shares of 6 per cent; the system now comprising 687 miles, with some 80 miles under construction or authorized. Judged by such tests, it could be said to stand about fourth among the railway companies of the United Kingdom.[11] In one very important respect, however, it ranked absolutely first. Its stock stood higher than that of any other major British railway company. In 1862 it was quoted at prices that varied between 126½ and 134½. Among its chief rivals the Great Northern stock just managed to touch the lowest Midland price, fluctuating from 113 to 126½. The London & North Western stood at 92-97½, the Great Western far below at 64-75¼.[12] Judged by this criterion, the Midland Railway was the most desirable property of them all.

In London, however the Company was little known – scarcely better than the Lancashire & Yorkshire, the North Eastern, or the Scottish companies. It was a provincial concern. That indeed was its strength. It was deeply rooted in the economic life of its territory, with its headquarters firmly fixed at Derby, presided over and managed by men of the Midlands. John Ellis, the Leicester Quaker, was succeeded as Chairman in 1858 by Samuel Beale of Birmingham, who gave place to another Leicester Quaker, W E Hutchinson, in 1864. The Company's brilliant General Manager, James

Allport, was the son of a Birmingham manufacturer of small arms. This might merely have connoted inbreeding, with complacency as a consequence. But these were men of vigour, foresight, and courage, who went out to meet the challenges of their time. They made up their minds slowly, with deliberation; but once they had decided that their company must make its own way to Manchester and London, they faced and overcame every obstacle in their path. And the second-rate would not do for them. If the provincial Midland Company was to set up for itself in the capital, it must do so on the grand scale. Their style of thinking is symbolized for us most impressively, perhaps, by the splendid public buildings designed in these years: by Brodrick's town hall at Leeds and Barry's at Halifax, by the warehouses that ennobled Manchester and Bradford in the 'fifties and early 'sixties.

Two men played an outstandingly important part in the making of the Midland Company's London extension: in the adoption of the plan and its passage through Parliament, the General Manager, James Allport; in its physical realization, W H Barlow, the Company's Consulting Engineer *(ills 2 and 3)*.

Allport had entered railway service as a clerk with the Brimingham & Derby Junction Railway at its inception in 1839. He was an early advocate of a Railway Clearing House and may be regarded as one of the founders of that institution. He served successively as Manager of the Newcastle & Carlington Junction and the Manchester Sheffield & Lincolnshire Companies and then went to the Midland in 1853. His first spell of office with the Company coincided exactly with the building of the Leicester & Hitchin line. That represented a policy he warmly supported, one of turning the Midland from a central connecting system into a major trunk railway in its own right. He then spent three years with a shipbuilding firm at Jarrow, before returning to the Midland Company in 1860. As soon as he came back he threw himself energetically into the project for a Midland line to Manchester. The first stage (Rowsley-Buxton) was sanctioned in 1860. In the following year he adroitly negotiated an agreement with the Manchester Sheffield & Lincolnshire Company, as a result of which the Midland was able to run its trains into Manchester, triumphant at last, in 1867. When he re-entered the Midland's service, Allport was not quite fifty. Abounding with energy and ideas, enterprising, cool-headed, courageous, he proved an outstandingly fine servant of his Directors and shareholders, and of British railway travellers at large.[13]

Barlow was a year younger than Allport. He too had served with one of the three small constituent companies of the Midland, the Midland Counties, and he moved on to become Chief Engineer of the amalgamated Company in 1844. He was responsible, among many other works, for the building of

2. William Henry Barlow (1812-1902)   *3. Sir James Allport (1811-92)*

the Leicester & Hitchin line. When it was completed in 1857 he set up in private practice in London, but he remained Consulting Engineer to the Midland Company to the end of his very long life. It was one of his chief merits that he was a ready and patient collaborator. In the years we are speaking of, he was working closely with John Hawkshaw on the completion of the Clifton Suspension Bridge. The significance of that association will appear presently.

He was a more systematic scientist than most railway engineers of this time, inheriting a predilection for research from his notable father Peter Barlow, Professor of Mathematics at the Woolwich Royal Military Academy. Several of his papers were published in the *Philosophical Transactions* of the Royal Society – of which he became a Fellow at the age of thirty-nine and a Vice-President in 1880. Three of these papers, in 1855-59, were concerned with the strength of beams; in 1867 he and his brother Peter William collaborated in a new edition of their father's *Treatise on the Strength of Materials.* He took a leading part in the introduction of steel into engineering structures from 1858 onwards. His interests were not narrowly confined to his profession. In 1868 he turned aside to produce an *Analytical Investigation of the Board of Trade Returns of the Capital and Revenue of Railways in the United Kingdom.* Research was indeed a passion with him, and he urged its claims powerfully upon his colleagues in his presidential address to the Institution of Civil Engineers in 1879. As a young man Barlow had been trained under Robert Stephenson, one of the two foremost railway engineers of the second generation. He himself was unquestionably among the leading men in the third.[14]

*   *   *   *

If the Midland was to build a line of its own to London, there could be little doubt about the route it should take. It must leave the Leicester and Hitchin line at Bedford, run south to Luton, and so reach London by way of St Albans and Hendon. This course was not by any means straight; but it had the advantage of occupying the territory in Bedfordshire, Hertfordshire, and Middlesex that lay between the two existing trunk lines to the north, offering Luton, St Albans, and Mill Hill a main-line service, instead of that provided by branches from the Great Northern. The route was not an ideal one. Its meandering meant that Bedford would be two miles further from the new London terminus than it was from King's Cross via Hitchin. Much more serious, the entry into London involved major engineering works: a tunnel at Elstree, a substantial viaduct over the River Brent, a longer tunnel just south of Hampstead Heath, and a complicated accumulation of difficulties over the last mile that will be described later.

The Midland Railway (Extension to London) Bill came before Parliament early in 1863. It was only to be expected that the Great Northern and London & North Western Companies would oppose it. But they were not alone. Among other bodies presenting petitions against it were the Metropolitan Board of Works and the St Pancras Vestry, the Regent's and the Grand Junction Canal Companies, and the Imperial Gas Light & Coke Company, whose gas-works had been established at St Pancras for forty years.[15] The Midland Company experienced no serious difficulty, however, in proving its case, on the grounds of the superior accommodation the line would bring to the country it traversed and of the relief it would offer from the intolerable delays, inconveniences, and expense involved in the existing arrangements. The Bill was not amended in any important matter during its passage through parliament,[16] and it became law on June 22nd.[17]

The Company was authorized by this Act to spend a maximum of £2,333,330 on the construction of the whole line, £1,750,000 of which were to be in shares, the remainder raised on loan. This sum proved quite inadequate for the purpose. Though it is impossible to compute precisely the total cost of the London Extension, it certainly exceeded, first and last, £5 million. Neither Allport nor Barlow could have imagined, victorious in that summer, that the whole work would take thirteen years to complete.

[1] Four histories of the Company have been written: F S Williams, *The Midland Railway* (1876); C E Stretton, *The History of the Midland Railway* (1901); C H Ellis, *The Midland Railway* (1953); and E G Barnes, *The Rise of the Midland Railway, 1844-74* (1966).

[2] The complicated history of the various projects for railways from Leicester southwards in 1845-53 is described most fully – though not always very clearly – in Barnes, *Rise of the Midland Railway*, 80-5, 140-4.

[3] Its construction and opening are described in some detail by Barnes: *ibid.*, 144-59.

[4] C H Grinling, *History of the Great Northern Railway* (1966 ed.), 165.

[5] *Ibid.*, 181. The main heads of the agreement are set out in Barnes, 163-4. The agreement, dated June 1, 1858, is scheduled to the Act authorizing the building of the coal depot: Local and Personal Act, 23 vict. cap. Lxvii.

[6] P.P. 1863, viii. 71.

[7] Sir H T Wood, *History of the Royal Society of Arts* (1913), 419.

[8] *Builder*, 9 August 1862, 565. In 1862 the Midland carried 38% more passengers to London (Euston and King's Cross) than in 1861.

[9] Barnes, 185.

[10] Geoffrey Cannon has shown that the decision was made by a small group of directors under the influence of James Allport, General Manager. 'A Nineteenth Century Investment Decision: the Midland Railway's London Extension', *Economic History Review*, 2nd series, 25 (1972), 448-70.

[11] It stood fourth in the length of its lines, after the London & North Western, the Great Western (including the West Midland and South Wales Companies, which were about to become fully merged with it) and the North Eastern; fourth in the receipts from its traffic (after the London & North Western, the Great Western, and the North Eastern): and third in the size of its capital – only the London & North Western and the Great Western exceeded it. (*Bradshaw's Railway Shareholder's Manual*, 1863, appendix, 44, 52, 56, 57, 58, 108.)

[12] *Bradshaw's Railway Shareholder's Manual*, 1863, 102.

[13] The fullest account of Allport's career is in M.P.I.C.E. 104 (1893), 390-5.

[14] The best biographical account of Barlow is in M.P.I.C.E 151 (1902-3), 388-400.

[15] They had been built under Parliamentary powers obtained in 1822.

[16] Except that the Midland Company withdrew the provisions concerning its junction with the Metropolitan Railway, to be submitted again in a future session.

[17] Local and Personal Act, 26 & 27 Vict., cap. lxxxiv.

CHAPTER II

Site and Plan

IF the Directors and officers of the Midland Company had pooled their collective experience with a view to securing a site for their London station that would combine the greatest possible number of difficulties, they could hardly have fixed on anything better than the one they chose at St Pancras. It was occupied by a canal, a gas-works, an ancient church with a large and crowded graveyard, and some of the most atrocious slums in London; and through it all ran the Fleet River (ill. 4).

The terminus was to face on the Euston Road (or the New Road, as it was then still called, even though it was over a hundred years old). Only half a mile away to the north it would be necessary for the railway to cross the Regent's Canal, which had opened in 1820, either by a bridge above or by burrowing underneath. If the station was on the level of the Euston Road, or below it, and the railway line passed under the canal, that would force trains to climb up a long and sharply-rising gradient almost as soon as they had started. Such a mistake had already been made at King's Cross next door, where the line rose through the Gas Works and Copenhagen Tunnels for over a mile at 1 in 107 – a standing cause of delay when the rails were greasy, as well as of unpleasantness for passengers and something much worse for engine-crews throughout the Age of Steam. Even as things were, when the line had been laid out to cross over the Canal and to end up some 15 feet above the level of the Euston Road, the Midland trains had to roar up through the Belsize Tunnel (a mile long) at 1 in 182. If the railway had passed underneath, a much steeper gradient than that would have been needed for some four miles continuously from the point of crossing.

A second difficulty was that the Midland line was intended to form a junction with the Metropolitan, the world's first underground railway, which had been opened from Paddington to Farringdon Street on January 10, 1863. Its tracks ran east and west in a tunnel a few feet below the Euston Road. If the station was to be raised up above the level of the road, then this junction line would have to pass beneath the station itself – and of course

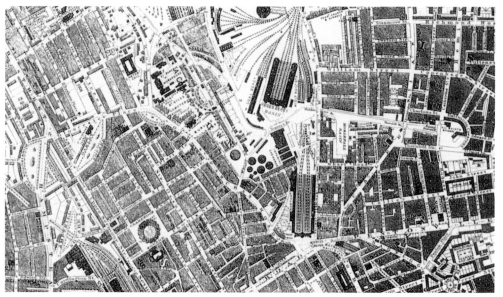

4. *Map of the St Pancras area before the station was built, taken from Stanford's map of 1862. King's Cross station is in the foreground with its hinterland of goods depots and marshalling yards to the rear. To the west of King's Cross lie the crowded streets shortly to be demolished for St Pancras station.*

beneath the Regent's Canal. The Company had it in mind to construct a double junction underground, to enable its trains to pass on to the Metropolitan line in both directions, east and west; but this idea met with the disapproval of the Inspecting Officer of the Board of Trade, Col. Yolland. He was convinced that it would be wrong to allow more traffic to flow on to the Metropolitan line from other railways unless its two tracks were increased to four. 'As at present constructed with two lines of railway,' he wrote, 'though exceedingly well adapted to supersede to a very great extent omnibus and cab traffic, it [the Metropolitan Railway] will not accommodate through passenger traffic.' Hence, while admitting that 'strong evidence may be produced in favour of this large Company to obtain a terminus in London', he advised against the proposed junction with the Metropolitan.[1] His advice was accepted. A simple plan was adopted in the following year, providing instead for access to the Metropolitan in an eastward direction only. Yolland put forward the same objection to this line,[2] but it was nevertheless authorized in 1864, with the specific proviso that it should not be opened until two additional tracks had been completed to Farringdon Street. It was an important gain for the Midland Company, offering it a through route into Kent by way of Snow Hill and the London Chatham & Dover

Railway, potentially useful for passengers and even more valuable for its coal traffic. With this advantage in prospect, the Company gave no warm support to two other schemes of this same year for underground lines linked with its own, running southwards to Charing Cross and the South Eastern Railway.[3]

The third obstacle to be overcome lay, once again, below the level of the ground. The Fleet River had been an important river in medieval London.[4] It had been covered over in 1825[5] and formed one of the city's principal sewers. It ran – it still runs – from its source on the heights of Hampstead under the Regent's Canal and exactly along the line of the western side of Pancras Road as it is now, on the way down to its outflow into the Thames by Blackfriars Bridge. In constructing its railway the Company had to take stringent precautions to preserve the sewer and its noisome contents from even the slightest damage.

The land to be occupied by the railway, its station and ancillary buildings, fell mainly within two districts called Somers Town and Agar Town, and within estates belonging to the Skinners' and the Brewers' Companies. Somers Town was an eighteenth-century creation, begun about 1790 on land leased from Lord Somers.[6] The houses were cheap, and when refugees from the French Revolution began to pour into the country they settled here in substantial numbers. One of them built a chapel in 1808 for his fellow-Catholics to worship in. They were buried, however, in the graveyard outside the ancient parish church of St Pancras.

St Pancras church and all its neighbourhood had been forlorn and dilapidated for centuries past. In Elizabeth's time John Norden had observed that 'about this church have been many buildings, now decayed, leaving poor Pancras without company or comfort'.[7] The church was shut down for a time after the completion of the new one on the Euston Road – Sir John Summerson's 'queen of early nineteenth-century churches'[8] – in 1822: but it was restored and partly rebuilt in 1847-48 to the designs of Roumieu and Gough (ill. 5).

The churchyard was venerable ground indeed, for this was the burial-place for much of north London. There had been chapels-of-ease, as at Kentish Town, for a long time past; but they had no rights of burial and so, as Norden remarked, when the inhabitants of these parts had a corpse to inter, 'they are forced to leave the same within this forsaken church or church-yard, where (no doubt) it resteth as secure against the day of resurrection as if it lay in stately Paul's'.[9] Many well-known people were buried here: Jeremy Collier, Jonathan Wild, Leoni the architect, Theobald the editor of Shake-speare, Paoli, the Chevalier d'Eon, William Godwin and his two wives. As the population living on and near the Euston Road grew, the churchyard

5. Old St Pancras Church in Pancras Road, as restored by Roumieu and Gough in 1847-8.

became appallingly overcrowded It was enlarged from its original 1½ acres to five in 1792. In the years that followed it received many French ecclesiastics, refugees living near by, headed by Archbishop Dillon of Narbonne. A further extension was made in 1803 as a burial ground for St Giles-in-the-Fields, and it was here in 1815 that Sir John Soane erected his idiosyncratic monument to his wife.

To reach the Euston Road from Kentish Town, the railway would either have to demolish the gas-works of the Imperial Gas Light and Coke Company or pass over the churchyard. The first alternative would be extremely costly and troublesome. The second was a great deal cheaper, but it proved to be troublesome too. The unfortunate proximity of the gas-works and the church-yard added materially to the difficulties the railway had to overcome, not only while it was being built but long afterwards.

To the north-west of Somers Town lay Camden Town (begun in 1791), and to the north, on the banks of the canal, Agar Town. This was a later development. If the Somers and Camden estates had been laid out with very modest houses, Agar Town was never anything but a slum from the first *(ill. 6)*. It was occupied by weekly tenants of extreme poverty, who had been displaced by the formation of New Oxford Street. 'The leases terminate at the end of 21 years', we are told, 'which have brought together such a variety of poor of every description . . . as to make it a second St Giles, it being very hazardous for any respectable dressed person to pass or repass without insult or annoyance.'[10] Moy Thomas gave an unforgettable description of the houses of Agar Town in the paper he called 'A Suburban Connemara', printed in Dickens' *Household Words* in 1851.[11] It was a shanty town, a morass of mud, fetid with disease. 'Every garden had its nuisance – so far the inhabitants were agreed – but every nuisance was of a distinct and peculiar character', wrote Thomas. 'In the one, was a dung-heap; in the next, a cinder-heap; in a third, which belonged to the cottage of a costermonger, was a pile of whelk and periwinkle shells, some rotten cabbage, and a donkey; and the garden of another, exhibiting a board inscribed with the words "Ladies' School", had become a pond of thick green water, which was carefully dammed up and prevented from flowing over upon

6. *'The Water Coming in at Agar Town', depicted in* The Builder *8 Oct. 1853.*

the canal towing-path by a brick parapet.' To summarize it all: 'In Agar Town we have, within a short walk of the City – not a gas-light panorama of Irish misery, "almost as good as being there", but a perfect reproduction of one of the worst towns in Ireland.'[12]

The site had been leased by William Agar in 1810-16. The freehold was attached to the Prebend of St Pancras in St Paul's Cathedral. (By an interesting coincidence, the Charing Cross Railway had just been the means of destroying a similarly dreadful slum by the Borough Market, on land belonging largely to the Archbishop of Canterbury and the Bishop of Winchester.) The Midland Company took a large part of Agar Town for its passenger and goods lines and obliterated it – so that, apart from Agar Grove, which passes over the railway a little north of the canal, and the tiny Agar Place leading off it, nothing remains to recall its horrors. In a brutal fashion, this was a real Metropolitan Improvement.[13]

For the building of the passenger station it was necessary to demolish the church of St Luke, which had recently been completed almost in the centre of the site, facing on to the Euston Road. By clause 83 of its Act of 1863 the Midland Company was obliged to provide the sum of £12,500 for the building of a new church. This was erected in 1868-69 in Oseney Crescent, Kentish Town. It was the first important commission of Basil Champneys.[14]

Seven streets were destroyed for the same purpose, with all their houses. The occupants were evicted, and though some of them fought strenuously to obtain compensation they were unsuccessful.[15] Their case came up on three occasions before Bloomsbury County Court.[16] The proceedings throw a clear, cold light on the attitude of the landlords (Messrs Mills and Perry) to their tenants. They were selling their property to the Midland Railway for £19,500 and offered to 'clear the people out' for a further payment of £200. The Company's solicitor accepted this proposal, saying that if it had not been made he would 'have given the tenants small sums by way of gratuity'.[17] Thereupon the landlords contended that this miserable £200 was a payment for their service to the Company 'and that the tenants had no right or title to any part of the money'. The court in the end felt obliged to uphold them. Having taken time for consideration Judge Russell concluded that, as the law stood, weekly tenants had no claim to compensation if they were evicted. He added that he 'felt the hardship of the tenants' case, and expressed his regret at the decision he was compelled to arrive at'. An estimated 4,000 houses were demolished by the company, leaving c. 32,000 people homeless.[18]

* * * *

Meanwhile Barlow and his staff were at work on the plans for the station. It was inevitable that they should be slow to attain their final form, for they had to furnish solutions to a most unusual conjunction of difficulties. They were determined by three considerations: the provincial Company's strong desire to impress itself upon London by a display of physical magnificence; the peculiar problems posed by the site it had chosen; the current practice of engineers and architects in designing similar works, in London and else-where. We have seen something of the first two of these factors. It is time now to turn to the third, to look at St Pancras in the perspective of the station-building of its time.

The terminal stations of the Midland Company's two chief rivals lay very close to its own site at St Pancras: Euston a quarter of a mile to the west, King's Cross adjoining it immediately to the east.

Euston was the earliest main-line terminus in London, brought into use in 1837. It had always been eccentric. It boasted the greatest monumental archway in England: a superb symbol, standing out in the open fields of the limitless vista of travel opened up by the railway to the North (ill. 7). In the Great Hall and Shareholders' Room, added in 1849, it included two of the most splendid rooms in London. For the rest, however, it can be said with-out much exaggeration that the mere passengers and railway men crept about

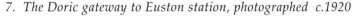

7. The Doric gateway to Euston station, photographed c.1920

8. King's Cross station, photographed c1890

like pygmies in the spaces between these giant creations. In spite of enlargement and a multiplication of platforms in 1848, and further alterations in 1851, the accommodation provided for the station's daily business remained inadequate.[19] By the 1860s, as the traffic grew, its deficiencies were becoming increasingly evident. Euston was suffering the common penalties of the pioneer in technological development: it pointed the way to the future and then, remaining static in its achievement, fell back into obsolescence.

King's Cross was newer and represented the very opposite ideas to those displayed so grandly at Euston *(ill. 8)*. It was – it remains up to the present moment – one of the most completely satisfying demonstrations in London of functionalism in architecture. It was designed by Lewis Cubitt in association with his brother Joseph and completed in 1852: a double train-shed, one-half for arrivals, the other for departures, with a booking-hall and offices on the departure side and a covered entrance for carriages in front; the whole encased in decent yellow brick, the arches of the sheds displayed in the façade, which was surmounted with a neat Italianate turret containing – what could be more useful to travellers? – a clock. Two years later, facing the booking-hall on the station's west side, the Great Northern Hotel was added, to an agreeable curved plan. The architect's uncle Sir William Cubitt was alleged to have remarked that 'a good station could be built at King's Cross for less that the cost of the ornamental archway at Euston Square'.[20] That was not achieved – the figure given for the cost of the station was £123,500 and that was admittedly too low, whereas the Euston Arch had cost £35,000. Nevertheless the Chairman felt justified in calling it 'the cheapest building for what it contains and will contain that can be pointed out in London'.[21] In its plainness and simplicity, King's Cross represented a standing rebuke to its ostentatious neighbour down the road at Euston.[22]

In the meantime the Great Western Company had embarked upon building itself a new station at Paddington, to the east of the original – a temporary wooden structure that had done duty since the line was opened in 1838. Here a plan appeared that was new to London and was adopted for several subsequent railway termini. As at Euston and King's Cross, the main entrance and booking-offices were at the side of the departure platform. The train-shed here was divided into three: a nave and two aisles, as it were, respectively 102 and 68 feet wide; and whereas the roofs of King's Cross had been made of laminated timber, those at Paddington were of iron and glass throughout, reflecting in some respects the great advance in design that had been demonstrated by the Great Exhibition building of 1851.

The innovation – an innovation, that is, in London, for it had already appeared at Hull and York[23] - lay in the placing of the hotel, transversely across the head of the station at the end of the platforms and fronting chiefly on to the street. The hotel was then more intimately a part of the station than it is today, when the buffer-stops have been pushed back to clear the circulating space always known to railwaymen as The Lawn.[24] In other respects, however, the station remains little altered. Some of the original office accommodation has gone, swept away in an air-raid; platforms have multiplied, and there has been a substantial addition to the arrival side of the station. But, as at King's Cross, the composition can still be seen and appreciated as a whole.

The plan of the station was laid down by the Company's Engineer, Brunel, and he took the main responsibility for it; but he persuaded his friend Matthew Digby Wyatt to act as his 'assistant for the ornamental details', and they worked together in this relationship throughout.[25] The Great Western Hotel was designed by P C Hardwick.

The next large station to be built in London was Victoria, which was brought into use in 1860-62. It represented no striking advance in design, and much of the original building has now disappeared. Its beautiful iron roof, on the Chatham side, designed by John Fowler, survives;[26] and J T Knowles's Grosvenor Hotel still interposes, bulky and handsome, between the Brighton side and Buckingham Palace Road.

Victoria was followed by two other stations that are critically important for our purpose: Charing Cross and Cannon Street, the West End and the City termini of the South Eastern Railway. They were authorized in 1859 and 1861 and were both under construction when the Midland Company's London extension was being planned. Charing Cross was opened for passenger traffic in 1864 *(ill. 9)*, Cannon Street two years later. Both followed the Paddington pattern, in that they incorporated hotels in the station; but both were roofed in a new way, in a single huge span. The bold engineer responsible for these two works was John Hawkshaw. He was assisted by two of the sons of Sir Charles Barry, architect of the Houses of Parliament: Edward Middleton Barry, who designed both the hotels, and John Wolfe Barry, then a very young man, who was Assistant Resident Engineer. Unhappily, both these roofs have gone. Part of the one at Charing Cross collapsed in 1905, and the whole was then replaced by a flat structure;[27] Cannon Street was wrecked during the Second World War – station, hotel, and all. Barry's grand hotel at Charing Cross still contains some of its original features, notably the richly-ornamented ceiling in the dining-room; but the merit of its elevation has been destroyed by the rebuilding of the two top storeys since the war.

Not every one approved of these very large erections. The *Building News*, for example, thought they were out of scale with their surroundings and

9. The trainshed at Charing Cross station, 1862-4

marred the London skyline. Paddington, Waterloo, and London Bridge stations served their purpose well enough, it argued. 'These enormous roofs are not required ... The necessity being disallowed, we regret the disfigurement, and repeat that it must have been but a careless exercise of power which permitted their existence in their present forms.'[28]

Wide though these roofs were, they did not outstrip all their predecessors. The span was 164 feet at Charing Cross, 190 feet at Cannon Street.[29] In the 1850s New Street station in Birmingham could already show a roof that, at its widest point, stretched to 211 feet. That was only one section of an irregular curved design for a station open at both ends. What Hawkshaw did was to make his two London stations, in effect, into single vast halls in iron and glass, completely screened from the streets outside by the massive brickwork and masonry of their hotels.

The new South Eastern termini represented the most up-to-date thinking in London that was relevant to the problems that Barlow and his colleagues had to face at St Pancras. Though Broad Street was also under construction, for the North London Company, in these years (it was authorized in 1861 and opened in 1865), it displayed no features of special interest in the connection. Outside London no major work, at all comparable in scale with St Pancras, was undertaken between Dobson's Newcastle station in the late forties and the third Lime Street station at Liverpool, which was not begun until 1867. The most striking contemporary work on the Continent was the second Gare du Nord in Paris (1861-65); but in so far as the problems it had to meet were similar to those encountered at St Pancras, the solutions adopted were different.

Hawkshaw and Barry offered general suggestions for the form of the station at St Pancras, which were of great value. It was particularly fortunate that, as we have seen, Barlow should have chanced to be working closely with Hawkshaw on the Clifton Bridge just at this time. He studied the plans of the South Eastern stations – and especially their roofing – with care, and he doubtless discussed them with their author. But that was all. From the outset the Midland station had to meet different needs from those of the South Eastern Company. Its business would be predominantly with long-distance traffic, and it would have to cater on a large scale for freight, either in the main station or in another close by, whereas Charing Cross and Cannon Street dealt with passengers only.

In working out the design of the roof Barlow had extended discussions with R M Ordish, one of the leading experts in Europe on iron construction of this type. Ordish had worked on the Crystal Palace, both in Hyde Park and at Sydenham, and on the roof of the Birmingham station in the fifties. He had also designed the roof of the Central station in Amsterdam for the

Dutch Rhenish Company – which much resembles that evolved for St Pancras, thought it is on a smaller scale. In later years he was to work with Gilbert Scott on the Leeds Infirmary and to design the roof of St Enoch Station in Glasgow *(cf. p.140)*. Barlow proclaimed his debt to Ordish at St Pancras most specifically: 'For the details of the roof', he wrote, he was 'indebted to Mr Ordish, whose practical knowledge and excellent suggestions enabled him, while adhering to the form, depth, and general design, to effect many improvements in its construction.'[30]

* * * *

The design of large stations was the subject of four major papers and discussions at the Institution of Civil Engineers between 1858 and 1870. These reflect both the experience gained with the pioneer stations of 1837-52 and that which was arising out of the second batch, beginning with Victoria. The engineers' argument ranged over a wide field of technical questions. Some concerned points of detail – was glazed earthenware to be preferred to slate in the construction of urinals, for example? But most of it dealt with large matters of planning. Where should the booking-offices be placed in relation to the platforms and waiting-rooms? Should they be at the head of the station, behind the buffers and as close as possible to the road outside, as at Fenchurch Street, Victoria (Brighton), and the two new South Eastern stations; or directly beside the main departure platform, as they were at King's Cross and Paddington? In the earlier stations it had been the practice to keep large numbers of carriages in sidings under the station roof. King's Cross, for example, as originally laid out, had two platforms only, one against the west wall for departures, the other against the east wall for arrivals. The whole of the intervening space was filled with sidings used for the accommodation of empty coaching stock. This made for flexibility and economy. The light carriages of the time could easily be manhandled from one line to another with the aid of the traversers or small round turntables that were provided. The carriages were readily at hand and could quickly be brought into use if a train needed strengthening to cope with a sudden influx of passengers. No less important, it saved unnecessary wear and tear on the vehicles. It was pointed out that at Waterloo, where very little such storage was provided, the carriages had to be taken four miles to be serviced.[31] The counter-argument is interesting: that by the 1860s the price of land in London was so greatly augmented that it was cheaper, for all the cost and inconvenience involved, to buy land for the accommodation of carriages and engines in the suburbs.[32]

But the biggest difference among the engineers arose over the design of roofs, and the planning that they reflected *(ill. 10)*. The huge single spans of Birmingham (New Street), of Charing Cross and Cannon Street, were adopted in order to eliminate internal columns, especially in view of an accident that had occurred at Bricklayers' Arms station, when a train had collided with one of these supports, bringing down a large part of the roof.[33] Robert Jacomb Hood, who had designed the Brighton Company's station at Victoria, still defended his own practice there, which was to use a two-span roof of the King's Cross type, guarding against any possibility of danger from similar collisions in the future by placing the line of columns in the roadway used for cabs. He gave figures – which were disputed – to show that the cost of his roof was far less than that incurred at Charing Cross and Cannon Street.[34]

* * * *

Barlow was a man of strong common sense, without petty vanity, always willing to take part in the discussions of his professional colleagues and to profit by them. But he was also, by this time, among the most experienced of living railway engineers. He knew his own mind and, as he fully recognized, he confronted at St Pancras a highly individual problem, arising out of a set of conditions that were unique. 'Problem' is the right word, and it is not too much to say that the solution he found for it was exactly the right one *(ills. 11-12)*. He explained it, in a paper given to his colleagues in 1870, with such luminous clarity that it would be a waste of time to try to improve on his own words:

> 'In consequence of the height of the rails above the ground level, a large space extending over the whole area beneath the station, was available. The original design was to fill this space with the material excavated from the tunnel of the St Pancras branch [i.e. the line down to the Metropolitan Railway], and it was contemplated to make the roof of the passenger station either in two or in three spans. But the station being bounded on the south by the Euston Road, on the east by the old St Pancras Road, and on the west by Brewer Street, and the difference of level being such as to admit of the construction of a lower floor with direct access to these streets, the position was deemed so valuable that it was determined by the directors to devote the whole area to traffic purposes, communication being made with the rails by means of hydraulic lifts. The special purpose for which this lower floor has been arranged is for Burton beer traffic; and in order to economize the space to the utmost, it was determined to use columns and girders, instead of brick piers and arches, making the distances between the columns the same as those of the warehouses, which were expressly

arranged for the beer traffic. Thus, in point of fact, the length of a beer barrel became the unit of measure, upon which all the arrangements of this floor were based.

'This decision led to a reconsideration of the question of roofing the station. It became obvious that, if intermediate columns were employed, they must be carried down through the lower floor, be about 60 feet in length, and of much larger diameter than the rest of the columns under the station. This would have necessitated the employment of different patterns in the girders, cross girders, and the plating of the lower floor, and have increased the price per ton for that portion of the ironwork, besides interfering with the economical distribution of the space. Moreover, these columns must have carried large areas of roofing in addition to the flooring, involving a greatly increased weight on the foundations, which must have been enlarged accordingly; and as some of them would necessarily have been placed on the tunnel of the St Pancras branch, special means and increased expense would have been required to carry the imposed weight at those places.

'On the other hand, it was seen that the floor girders across the station formed a ready-made tie sufficient for an arched roof crossing the station in one span; all that was required to obtain a roof of this construction being the arch or upper member of the truss, of which the floor girders would form the lower member. There was third feature in the case. In iron roofs as usually constructed, the depth of the principal is about one-fifth of the span; but here, by adopting one arch extending across the station, the height from the tie beneath the rails to the crown of the arch became the effective depth of the truss; and this height being about two-fifths of the span, all the horizontal strains arising from the dead weight of the roof, its covering, and accumulations of snow, etc., would be about the same in the arch of 240 feet span, with an effective depth of truss of 100 feet, as in an ordinary truss of 120 feet span with a depth of 24 feet. Excepting, therefore, such additions as might be necessary for retaining the form and figure of the arch, the actual sectional area at the crown, and for about two-thirds of the entire arch, did not require to be greater than in an ordinary truss of 120 feet span. There were several other advantages belonging to the arch, – one being that as the weight of the roof was carried at the floor line, and did not rest on the tops of the walls, there was no necessity to make the side walls thicker, for not only was the weight on the tops of the walls avoided, but also the racking motion from the expansion and contraction of an ordinary roof, which, though it may be mitigated, is not prevented by the use of roller-frames at the feet of the principals, and appliances of a like nature. It was also apparent, that the arch might be made of rivetted

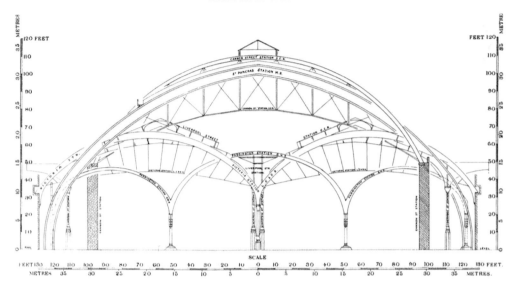

10. *Diagram of station roofs, from Arthur T Walmisley,* Iron Roofs *2nd edn, 1888*

11. *Section through St Pancras trainshed. Contract drawing no. 6, 1866*

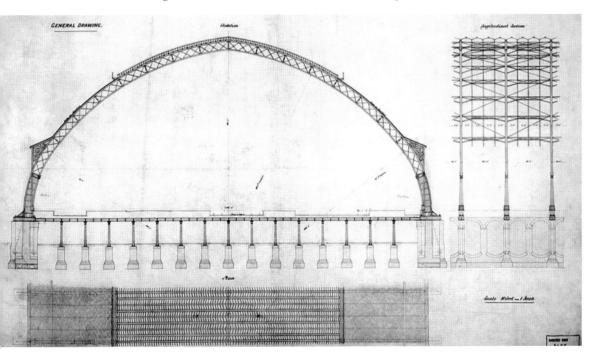

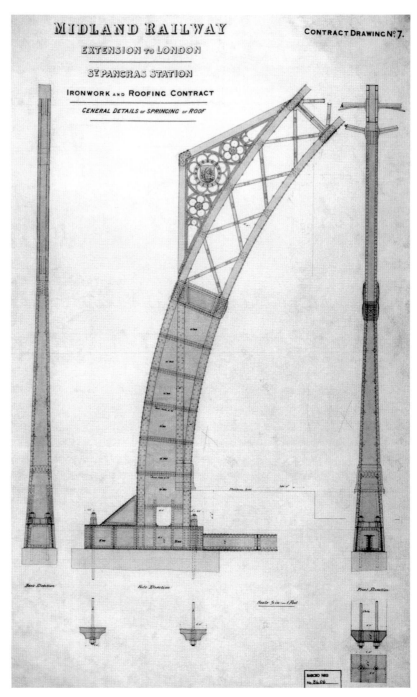

12. *General details of springing of roof. Contract drawing no. 7, 1866*

plate ironwork like that of an ordinary railway bridge, and the expense attending the use of forged and wrought work as in ordinary roofs would be avoided, including the screw-cutting, gibs and cotters, welding, and similar costly workmanship. Again, as to the question of the expansion and contraction of the arched roof, the ties being beneath the ballast, the temperature would vary so little, that no provision would be necessary; and for the arched part of the roof, which would alone be subject to appreciable change, the only effect would be a slight rise or fall in the crown.

'All the arrangements of roller-frames or slings, required in ordinary roofs to provide for the effect of variations of temperature, would, therefore, be avoided by the adoption of the arch; and lastly, the adoption of a single arch would not only save the cost of the columns and their foundations, but also that of the longitudinal girder required to connect them at their upper extremities, with a valley drain between the roofs, and vertical drain pipes, and other provisions for taking off the water from the area, between the centre lines of the two roofs, which would have been about two acres.'[35]

One famous feature of the St Pancras roof, which differentiated it from its predecessors, was its pointed crown. The design was adopted to afford the greatest possible protection against the lateral action of wind, although Barlow added that it also improved 'the architectural effect'.[36]

There was yet another element, a strictly economic one, in Barlow's exposition of the case for the single-span roof at St Pancras. He reserved it until he was nearing the close of his paper:

'When, therefore, it is considered that the Company obtained their station in the metropolis at such great cost for land and works; that its total area, in reference to the extent of railway, is less than that of any of the other important metropolitan termini, and that the Midland system is not yet in communication with all its expected sources of traffic, the sacrifice of a width of 5 feet or 6 feet, for the entire length of the most valuable part of the working space of the station, could hardly have been justified even if the saving had been greater than is estimated. As the station has been built, the whole working area is free from obstruction of any kind, and the Company may make any alterations in the arrangements of the lines and platforms which may from time to time best suit their large and growing traffic.'[37]

This powerful accumulated reasoning carried conviction with it. In the discussion that followed Barlow's paper, though his fellow-engineers took issue with him on minor points, none disputed the correctness of the chief decisions he had taken.

The planning of the station as a whole represents a feat of concentrated thinking about the requirements of traffic and the convenience of passengers. The beer-vault, with its easy access by a hydraulic lift, lowering wagons from the rails near the head of what is now No. 4 platform, is one striking example. Another is the system of access for road vehicles bringing passengers to and from the station. The flows of traffic arriving and departing were separated entirely. Empty cabs had their own access to the street on the departure side. Passengers arriving at the two chief platforms (now Nos. 5 and 6 – No. 7 was 'the excursion platform'[38]) stepped straight into the waiting vehicles and were driven away down the ramp into the Euston Road. Even now, when these arrangements have been modified and taxis wait elsewhere, the broad road along the platform is an invaluable feature.

It was the station alone that Barlow was concerned with. From the beginning the Midland Company had intended that there should also be an hotel at St Pancras. When, in 1868, this policy was for a time unpopular with a substantial section of the shareholders the Chairman (W E Hutchinson) explained, defensively, that the Directors had taken this decision in order to place their Company 'upon a par with the Great Northern, the London & North Western, and the Great Western. It was at that time, at all events, considered that these companies received a large accession of traffic from the construction of their hotels.'[39] Wise or unwise, the decision was fundamental to the planning of the new terminus.

Barlow fully accepted the principle that the station should be designed separately from the hotel and that the hotel should be the work of an architect, as at Charing Cross and Cannon Street. The station was plainly the more urgent work, and it had the priority. Barlow determined the ground area that the hotel was to occupy, at some day in the future. His responsibility ended there. His plans for the station, including its bold single-span roof, were accepted by the Committee at a series of meetings in the spring of 1865. At the last of these, on May 3rd, the Committee decided to hold a limited competition among architects for the design of the station buildings and hotel.[40] These buildings were to include provision for the office accommodation required in order to enable the headquarters of the Midland Railway to be transferred from Derby to London; a removal that, if it had actually taken place, might have materially altered the character of the Company. That proposal, as we shall see, was soon dropped. The competition, and the construction that followed closely upon it, will be considered in their place later in the story.

[1] P.P 1863, lxii, 848,853.

[2] *Ibid.*, 1864, liii,905.

[3] These were the Charing Cross Northern and the Tottenham & Hampstead Junction (Extension to Charing Cross) Railways: *ibid.*, 884-5,907-8.

[4] Cf. N. J. Barton, *The Lost Rivers of London* (1962, rev. ed. 1992), chap.ii

[5] *Survey of London*, xxiv (1952), 102.

[6] Ibid., 118-23.

[7] *Speculum Britanniae* (1593), quoted in A J C Hare, *Walks in London* (1878), ii, 144.

[8] *Georgian London* (1945), 203.

[9] Quoted in P Cunningham, *Handbook for London* (1849), 619.

[10] J F King (*c* 1850), quoted in *Survey of London*, xix (1938), 61.

[11] *Household Words* contributors' book: Parrish Collection, Princeton University Library.

[12] *Household Words* 2 (1851), 564, 565.

[13] Steven L J Denford has argued that Agar Town 'was not the hell-hole of contemporary description'. 'Agar Town: Life and Death of a Victorian Slum', *Occasional Papers of the Camden History Society* (1995), 22.

[14] *Survey of London*, xxiv (1952), 143.

[15] The demolition of houses for the building of railways is well dealt with by H. J. Dyos in 'Railways and Housing in Victorian London': *Journal of Transport History* 2 (1955-56), 11-21, 90-100.

[16] *Builder*, 23 December 1865, 914.

[17] Offers of this sort were common in such cases at the time: cf. Dyos, *loc. cit.*, 95-6.

[18] *The Working Man*, 8 Sept. 1866, 109.

[19] [G R Smith,] *Old Euston* (1938), 26-7.

[20] Grinling, 114.

[21] *Ibid.*, 124.

[22] John Summerson, *Victorian Architecture. Four Studies in Evaluation* (1970), 25-36.

[23] Cf. M J Minett, 'The Railway Stations of George Townsend Andrews', *Journal of Transport History*, 7 (1965-66), 47, 49, 50-1.

[24] That space was re-ordered in 1997-9.

[25] Brunel to Wyatt, January 13, 1851: L T C Rolt, *Isambard Kingdom Brunel* (1957), 232.

[26] It is described and illustrated in W Humber, *Record of the Progress of Modern Engineering* (1863).

[27] Since replaced by an air rights office building constructed over the platforms.

[28] *Building News*, 26 October 1866, 705. This leading article goes on to make a slashing attack on the ornamentation of the Cannon Street Hotel.

[29] The roofs are described and illustrated in Humber, *op. cit.* (1865 and 1868).

[30] M.P.I.C.E. 30 (1869-70), 82. At the opening of the station 'Mr Barlow stated publicly that the design of this roof was Mr Ordish's' (*Engineer*, 17 September 1886, 233).

[31] M.P.I.C.E. 25 (1865-66), 269.

[32] M.P.I.C.E. 25 (1865-66), 285.

[33] *Ibid.*, 266.

[34] M.P.I.C.E. 27 (1867-68), 433-4.

[35] M.P.I.C.E. 30 (1869-70), 79-81.

[36] *Ibid.*, 84.

[37] M.P.I.C.E. 30 (1869-70), 90.

[38] P.P. 1892, lxix, 209.

[39] *Railway Times* 31 (1868), 52.

[40] PRO, RAIL 491/280, min.101.

CHAPTER III

Construction

The Board of Directors of the Midland Company entrusted the over sight of the new line, and all the works on it, to a special sub-committee from the outset. It began life on March 2, 1864 as the Bedford to London Construction Committee and was renamed the South Construction Committee on September 5, 1864. For the sake of simplicity, the second title will be used here throughout.[1] It normally met twice a month, and its minutes enable us to follow the progress of the railway, the station, and the hotel, often in meticulous detail. Moreover the London works were spectacular enough – with the crossing of the churchyard lending a touch of the macabre to them – to attract substantial attention from the press. All in all, we probably have fuller written evidence for the building of St Pancras than we have for any other London station: though, alas, there is nothing here that can be compared with the marvellous drawings in which J C Bourne recorded, sometimes almost day by day, the building of Euston.

The responsibility for the 49¾-mile line was apportioned between two chief engineers: Barlow for the southern section, to a point 14½ miles from London, Charles Liddell for the remainder, on to Bedford. The work was divided into nine contracts. From 1 mile 70 chains north of the Euston Road the contractors were Joseph Firbank, Waring Bros, and Thomas Brassey.[2] The southernmost part was divided into two sections, the shortest but much the most difficult. That from 60 chains to 1 mile 70 chains went to A W Ritson. The ninth contract, from 60 chains (just north of the Regent's Canal) to the Euston Road, included the building of the passenger station and of the line that burrowed underneath it to join the Metropolitan Railway. It was itself sub-divided. The work required for the roof was so specialized and exacting that it was separated from the general contract and put out to tender on its own.

These two contracts needed the most complex preparatory work, and they were the last to be let. The Committee considered the main one – excluding the roof – on November 15, 1865. Barlow's estimate of what the work would cost was £310,000. Only one of the six tenders submitted came within that amount – that of George Wythes, at £306,396. (The highest, from C T Lucas, was £353,892.) Accordingly, Wythes was awarded the contract.[3] In three weeks' time, however, he was asking to be released from it. He seems to have got cold feet. The reason he gave for withdrawing was that 'the traffic on the Regent's Canal was likely to be affected': palpably an excuse, for he knew that when he tendered.[4]

This was one piece of bad luck for the Company, and it nearly fell into another, much worse. The next lowest tender was that of A W Ritson, and Barlow was instructed to ask if he would take the contract. He evidently declined. That was as well for every one, since he was already in difficulties with the other contract he held, which had to be removed from his hands and re-let in the following March.[5] Had he taken on the St Pancras one he would certainly have failed. As it was, Wythes's contract passed to Waring Bros, who had submitted the next lowest tender, at a little more than £319,000.[6] They carried the work through admirably. Though they were in trouble a year later with their other contract, further north, and had to relinquish it to Firbank,[7] through all the storms that were to come at St Pancras there were hardly any suggestions of delay attributable to them, and none at all of unsatisfactory workmanship.

The complementary contract, for the roof, was not let until July 18, 1866. Barlow's estimate was £121,000, and again only one tender came within it: that of the Butterley Company, whose price was just under £117,000. The other four ranged upwards to £144,500. The Butterley Company was an old-established and famous Derbyshire firm of good repute, an important customer of the Midland Railway. The Committee had every reason to award it the contract. No doubt it did so with a sense of relief.[8]

Both the contracts, with Waring Bros and the Butterley Company, have been preserved, and they run to a common pattern.[9] In both, for example, it is stipulated that no work shall be undertaken on Sundays unless the Company's Engineer shall certify that it is absolutely necessary, and that 'the Company shall have power to dismiss summarily any man found at work on a Sunday except under such certificate'. Both prohibit the contractors from retailing any provisions to their workmen. The tommy shop was still an evil memory.

Special precautions were written into the Warings' contract for the crossing of St Pancras churchyard (clauses 8-12). It was specified that the stone used in their work was to be either Derbyshire gritstone or Bramley Fall – which is quarried between Leeds and Otley and had already been used in a classic work of railway architecture, the Euston Arch.[10] The wrought-iron work was all to be of Derbyshire iron. The contractors agreed to complete the masonry and brickwork by June 1, 1867 and the remainder so that the railways could be inspected and approved by the Board of Trade not later than the following December 1st. The exact contract price was £319,162 4s 9d.

The Butterley contract is undated. The specification required the wrought iron to be made of Yorkshire or Derbyshire iron; the timber to be Memel, Riga, or Dantzic red pine, except for the planks and battens, which were to be of the best yellow Christiania or Petersburgh deals. It was laid down that the slate used should be 'best Welsh', in equal quantities of four different sizes (clause 59). This enabled the largest to be laid at the foot of the roof and the smallest at the top – something like the traditional grading that helps to give beauty to an old slate roof but was very unusual with mass-produced Welsh slates in the mid-Victorian age.[11] Work was to begin on September 1, 1866, proceeding from the south end of the station northwards; the first principal of the roof was to be erected by November 1, 1866 and then it was to be finished at the rate of one bay a week. The contract price was £116,720 7s 9d. the total of the two contracts, for the whole station (excluding the hotel), was thus £435,882 12s 6d.

Schedules of prices are appended to both contracts, and these include wage rates. Where both firms were employing men of the same trade, the Butterley Company's wages were usually higher. The rates for a day's work (defined as of ten hours in the Butterley contract) are shown in the table at the foot of the next page. For a cart with one horse and its driver Warings' specified 12s a day, for a two-horse cart 21s.

• • • •

Work began on the London extension at Kentish Town in the autumn of 1864.[12] the complex preparations, and the delay caused by Wythes's withdrawal meant that Waring Bros could not move in to tackle their formidable contract for the station until the spring of 1866. At the outset of the whole undertaking the Midland Board had adopted a schedule of construction that envisaged the opening of the line from Bedford as far as Cricklewood in the summer of 1867, thence to the goods station on the north of the Agar Town site a few months later, and the passenger station in the summer of 1868.[13] The whole of the gigantic work (including the complicated line tunnelling down to join the Metropolitan) had therefore to be completed, if time was to be kept, in a little over two years. The start was much later than had been intended; but a most determined effort was made, both by the Midland Company and by Warings, to see that as much as possible of the lost time was recovered. Through all that followed, it is important to remember that the work was being pressed forward against the clock.

44

The first tasks tackled were the construction of a temporary bridge over the Regent's Canal, to enable a contractor's railway to be carried the whole length of the site, and the clearing of the ground. The bridge was erected very fast – it was reported to be 'nearly finished' in the first week of March.[14] The demolition of the horrible Agar Town was carried through in March and April, followed by that of a great part of Somers Town in May and June. The delicate and difficult task of crossing the burial ground had then to be undertaken.

This was governed by the careful stipulations laid down in the Acts of 1863 and 1864. The main line was to be carried over the burial ground by a girder bridge, of two or three spans. The Branch was to burrow beneath it in a tunnel, whose crown was to be not less than 12 feet below the surface of the graveyard. Provision was made for the re-burial of the corpses disturbed, at the Company's cost, under the supervision of the Bishop of London or his agent and the Medical Officer of Health for the parish of St Pancras. The Company did its best to enforce these conditions on Warings by clauses in its contract. No doubt this was as far as Parliament and a railway company could be expected to go. But the provisions were quite inadequate for their purpose, to ensure decent treatment of the bodies in the burial ground – which had been in use until quite recently; and some scandal resulted, for which the Midland Company naturally bore the blame.

The Company authorized the appropriation of land in its possession for the re-burial of the bodies in June,[15] and the work went on through the autumn and winter of 1866-67, enabling first the contractors' timber bridge to

Trade	Waring	Butterley
Labourers (Waring contract: 'navigators or labourers')	4s 6d	5s 2½d
Bricklayers, masons, carpenters, smiths	7s 6d	
Smiths		8s 6d
Strikers (i.e. hammermen)	4s	5s 6d
Fitters	10s	8s 6d
Boys	3s 6d	4s 2d
Miners	8s	
Platelayers	6s	
Plumbers		8s 4d
Slaters and glaziers		7s 11d
Rivetters		8s

be built, secondly the tunnel for the Branch, and thirdly the permanent iron viaduct for the main line.

It is easy to see that, at the outset, the work was performed roughly and carelessly. On June 13th the Vicar of St Pancras, the Rev. Mr Arrowsmith, stated that he had seen many graves open in the burial ground, with dead men's shanks and skulls thrown about or placed in open boxes. When one coffin was stove in by a workman's spade, 'a fair bright tress of hair' appeared. Urged by the Bishop of London and a Parliamentary question, the Home Secretary sent an inspector to investigate, under the terms of the Burials Act, and he stopped all further work until the new ground had been prepared for the re-interment.[16]

When it came to the tunnelling operation, it was impossible for the work to be undertaken satisfactorily. The reasons were given, with revolting lucidity, by R L Roumieu, one of the architects who had been concerned with the reconstruction of old St Pancras church twenty years before.[17] In the course of that work, he wrote, they took in part of the graveyard. The clay was 'so saturated with decomposition as to be horribly foetid. The ordinary excavators who undertook the work deserted it, being made sick, although frequently given spirits by the contractors to prevent nausea; and their place was supplied by some seasoned gravediggers who were collected for this purpose.' Coffin was found piled upon coffin, with no more than the thinnest layers of clay between them. The proposed tunnel, Roumieu said, would be cut through the pits that had been used in the past for pauper burials. 'As the water was only kept down in them while they were open by constantly baling the interstices between the coffins, and being full of water, you may imagine the pleasant dropping which will take place through the very pervious arching which forms the roofs of most tunnels, when this reservoir of decomposition overlies the top of it.' He argued therefore that the whole project was not only irreverent but grossly insanitary – indeed dangerous at a time when a new attack of cholera threatened.

Roumieu's protest was unavailing. The tunnel went forward in spite of it. But the supervision of the work was now made much more strict. It was allowed, even by an unfriendly critic, that 'the removal appears to have been effected with great care, and with as much reverence as the case would admit of'.[18] The person appointed by Bishop Tait of London to supervise the execution of the work was the son of his predecessor: Arthur Blomfield, then rising into reputation as an architect. Blomfield engaged a clerk of works, whose duty it was to be on the spot at all hours at which the removal of bodies was taking place and to watch the way in which the task was performed. To keep the clerk of works up to scratch he instructed one of his own young assistants to call in irregularly, without notice; and to ensure that neither the clerk of works nor his assistant was lax, he would arrive himself from time to time without warning. The assistant he chose was Thomas Hardy.

Hardy was then twenty-six and had been working in Blomfield's agreeable office – where, in order to help on their tasks, they sang glees and catches, led by Blomfield himself – for four years. All through that autumn he visited the St Pancras burial ground daily, sometimes more than once.

> 'There after nightfall, within a high hoarding that could not be overlooked, and by the light of flare-lamps, the exhumation went on continuously of the coffins that had been uncovered during the day, new coffins being provided for those that came apart in lifting, and for loose skeletons; and those that held together being carried to the new ground on a board merely; Hardy supervising these mournful processions when present, with what thoughts may be imagined, and Blomfield sometimes meeting him there. In one coffin that fell apart was a skeleton and two skulls. He used to tell that when, after some fifteen years of separation, he met Arthur Blomfield again and their friendship was fully renewed, among the latter's first words were; "Do you remember how we found the man with two heads at St Pancras?"'[19]

Hardy was not the man to forget such macabre experiences. They are surely echoed in poems he wrote much later in his life – in *The Levelled Churchyard*, above all perhaps in the sixth of the *Satires of Circumstance*, 'In the Cemetery':

> 'And then the main drain had to cross,
> And we moved the lot some nights ago,
> And packed them away in the general foss
> With hundreds more. But their folks don't know,
> And as well cry over a new-laid drain
> As anything else, to ease your pain'

'The railway is no respecter of persons, living or dead', wrote Frederick Miller shortly after this time in his history of the parish of St Pancras. 'In its march it had levelled a town which ought never to have been built, and therefore was a benefactor; but in disturbing the remains of those who had been interred in the "sure and certain hope of a glorious resurrection", the feelings of survivors have been shocked, and their faith in such institutions almost destroyed'.[20] The memory of this unhappy business lived long. When in 1874 the Midland Company sought to acquire the rest of the burial ground (including the old church), its plans were fiercely opposed,[21] and thwarted. Another fifteen years went by before the Company could secure anything more; and then it was permitted to annex only a part of the south-eastern corner of the burial ground, for the price of £12,000.[22] The railway company was the loser by the opposition it aroused: for it was left with land of a very inadequate width for the expansion its business came to require at the entrance to the station. In the very long run it might have been worth its while to incur the great cost of buying up and demolishing the gas-works, on the eastern side of the line, instead.

The work of re-burying the bodies took a long time. It was not finished until March 1867.[23]

*   *   *   *

The building of St Pancras station could hardly have got under way in more anxious conditions. Railway property had not been notably prosperous in 1865 or in the early months of 1866. The general uneasiness was much increased when, in April 1866, the greater part of the Ordinary stock of the London Chatham & Dover Company was advertised to be sold at a slashing discount. [24] Several contractors were beginning to find it difficult to se-cure the advances they needed for the steady continuance of their work. and then, on May 10th, the great bill-discounting house of Overend Gurney & Co. stopped payment. 'No single bankruptcy, perhaps, ever caused so great a shock to credit', commented the *Annual Register*.[25] Some good observers had for some time been aware that the firm was unsound; but to the general public the news came like a sudden clap of thunder.[26] Bank rate was raised to 10 per cent, and held there for more than three months. Several provincial banks failed. All the rumbling unease among railway shareholders now burst out, often in frenzied complaint against those who managed their affairs. And not without reason: in the course of that year and the next, four major railway companies in England – the Brighton (hitherto a prosperous and well-conducted concern), the Chatham, the Great Eastern, and the Great Western – and the North British in Scotland were shaken to their foundations. The most celebrated of railway contractors, Sir Samuel Morton Peto, failed, together with many others in his line of business, like Thomas Savin in mid-Wales. At the same time came other calamities: the worst outbreak of cholera since 1854 – it proved particularly severe in the slums of St Pancras; a bad harvest, which made that winter a time of suffering for the poor, including many of those small investors who had been ruined, or at least very hard hit, by the financial disaster of the summer.

The nerve of the Midland Company's management was now put to the test indeed. No railway company had, at this moment, given more hostages to fortune. The new line to Manchester was nearing completion, the London extension was half built, St Pancras station had just started, and in the North the Company had at this very time a Bill before parliament for the construction of the formidably expensive railway from Settle to Carlisle. The Company fell for a little while into arrears in meeting its engineers' certificates in respect of the work undertaken by the contractors on the London extension.[27] It was fortunate to be dealing with men of the stature of Thomas Brassey, Joseph Firbank, and the Waring Brothers. The whole work could have been gravely delayed by the failure of one of them, when the best hope it had of extricating itself from its difficulties lay in the rapid completion of the line so that it could begin to earn a revenue. The Company weathered the first storm in the summer of 1866, but it soon became clear that there was much more trouble to come.

Work on the station forged ahead steadily, without interruption. The site was completely cleared by June, and in July the laying of the foundations began. These included 688 brick piers for carrying the cast-iron columns supporting the ironwork that formed both the roof of the beer-vault and the floor of the passenger station. By the middle of October 1866, 988 men were employed under the Warings, with 47 horses and 18 steam engines, one of them a locomotive.[28] Five months later these numbers had increased to 1,229 men and 111 horses; four locomotives were at work, and 18 other steam engines. Over two-fifths of the cellarage under the station was then complete, and the side walls had been begun (ill. 13).[29]

The St Pancras Branch, running down from St Paul's Road Junction to tunnel under the passenger station and join the Metropolitan Railway, was proceeding faster. It was the Company's intention to complete it as early as possible, in order to run a passenger service on to the Metropolitan line before its own terminal station was open. The work was complicated not only by the tunnelling through the burial ground, already mentioned, but by the crossing of Pancras Road and the treatment of the Fleet River. The cholera epidemic then raging in London lent especial point to the requirement, laid down by the Metropolitan Board of Works, that the Fleet should be entirely enclosed in a huge iron pipe. This difficult task was carried through in the closing weeks of 1866, and by the middle of January 1867 it was complete.[30] Since the Fleet had been for many years nothing but a sewer, the final enclosure of this section of it could be reckoned another important contribution that the building of the station made to the improvement of the health of north London.

This job finished, Warings' men turned to the railway tunnel, which proved an easier proposition than Roumieu had predicted. The work went ahead relatively smoothly throughout 1867, to a plan that provided for its completion and the opening of the line in January 1868 (ill. 14).

13. Photograph of St Pancras works, showing the cast-iron columns of the undercroft.

14. View of the works from the south-east corner; Illustrated London News, *15 Feb 1868.*

The other parts of the great undertaking made irregular progress. The supply of bricks and other materials gave constant trouble.[31] Worse still was the failure of the Butterley Company to adhere to the timetable provided for in its contract. The work on the roof should have gone in step with Warings' on the foundations and side walls. It had, however, fallen lamentably behind.

The Butterley Company had hardly signed their contract before they were warning the Midland Engineer that there was likely to be some delay in the delivery and erection of the first principal, to which the Committee answered that it relied on the time being recovered before the contract was complete.[32] This confident optimism proved sadly ill founded. By May 1867 the Warings' contract had progressed so far that six of the springers for the main ribs of the roof were in place; but it was not until November that the first section of any of the ribs was hoisted into position – just over a year later than the date provided for in the contract.[33] The Engineer and the Committee grew more and more indignant at the Butterley Company's slowness. By July 1867 the Midland's solicitors were writing to make formal complaints. They were writing again in November.[34]

The truth seems to be that the Butterley Company, experienced though it was in ironworking, had gravely underestimated the magnitude of the task if had undertaken. The roof was to be erected with the aid of a vast timber scaffold, of the same size as the opening of the train-shed, which was to move on rails as the work progressed from one bay to the next. Even this preliminary piece of equipment was not completed until the autumn of 1867 (ills 15-16).[35]

The Butterley Company's delays were not due solely to the unexpected technical difficulties of the task, or to its own dilatoriness.[36] The year 1867 was one of very great trouble for all commercial undertakings, and the Company had its share of it. The Midland's own position deteriorated gravely; the anxiety felt by some of its shareholders in the second half of 1866 became alarm in the following year. It found forceful expression in June 1867 in a pamphlet entitled *The Midland Railway: a Word to the Shareholders*, written anonymously by one of them.[37] The Company's capital, it pointed out, had been increased from £21 million to £30 million since 1860; its dividends had fallen;[38] expenditure in the future – especially on St Pancras station – was bound to exceed the estimates. It was likely, the writer argued, that the London extension would cost in the end not £1¾ million, the sum authorized by the Act of 1863, but more than £3 million. A committee of investigation ought to be set up 'to examine into the whole financial system and to stop a policy which can have but one result, that of ruin to us all'.

This attack was answered a fortnight later in *The Midland Railway: Another Word to the Proprietors, by a Larger Shareholder*,[39] who observed that 'in

15. *The station roof under construction, 1868, showing the timber scaffold which could be moved on wheels as work progressed.*

16. *Interior of roof during erection, 1868.*

ordinary times [the earlier pamphlet] would only have been noticed for the ignorance it displays, [but it] has had the effect of lowering the price of our Ordinary stocks in one week to the amount of about £750,000'. The writer went on to point out that as soon as St Pancras station could be completed and opened the Midland Company would be freed at a stroke from the tolls it was paying to the London & North Western and Great Northern Companies for sending its trains to London on their lines – a matter of £180,000 a year – and concluded by proving, at least to his own satisfaction, that the Midland was 'a sound commercial enterprise'.

The reply was effective; but it could not gainsay the evident truth that, at a time of so much danger, the Midland Company had too many expensive ventures on hand for safety. Among the shareholders the demand for retrenchment grew stronger – and stronger still after the Board had given notice (in December 1867) of its intention to raise another £5 million of capital, over £2 million of it being required for the London extension. They urged insistently that the Settle & Carlisle line should be given up. To this end one group of them even went so far as to form themselves into a Midland Shareholders' Association and negotiate privately with the London & North Western Railway Company in the matter, for which they were, very properly, disavowed by the body of the Company's shareholders as a whole. But the Directors came to the same broad conclusion, and in January 1868 they announced a policy of rigid economy, one element in which was to be an application to Parliament for leave to abandon the Settle & Carlisle line. They also accepted the appointment of a Consultative Committee of nine shareholders, under the chairmanship of Edward Baines, MP, proprietor of the *Leeds Mercury*. This committee, having investigated the Company's affairs, came to the conclusion that they had been well conducted, whilst opining that the Board had 'suffered the Company to be drawn into engagements far beyond what could be properly undertaken at any one time'.[40] Later in the spring, however, Parliament declined to grant the Midland Company's request, under pressure from the Midland's partners in the Settle & Carlisle enterprise, the Lancashire & Yorkshire and North British Companies, which stood to lose scarcely anything and to gain almost as much as the Midland from its completion. The costly work – the capital authorized to be raised for it was £2,200,000; it cost in the end just over half as much again – had therefore to proceed.

We should not underestimate the risks that these railway directors ran. Insolvency was no remote, inconceivable fate for a railway company that overplayed its hand: the London Chatham & Dover Company had gone bankrupt in 1866, the Great Eastern did likewise just a fortnight after that agitated shareholder wrote his pamphlet. It heightens our appreciation of the grandeur of the building we are considering to realize that its serene self-assurance represents an act of unshaken faith, carried resolutely through in conditions of anxiety, and at times of real danger, until it reached its appointed end.

Merchandise traffic began to be carried up the new line from Bedford to the goods station at Agar Town on September 9, 1867. The Midland management hoped it would be possible to send passenger trains through the tunnel on to the Metropolitan line by the beginning of 1868; but as that time approached it became plain that the Metropolitan would not be ready to receive them. In November Allport was instructed to write to complain of the backwardness of the Metropolitan's works, at the same time informing the Board of Trade that its own line would be ready for opening to passenger traffic on January 1st.[41] In February the Metropolitan was saying that it would not be able to take the Midland trains until May.[42] In fact the service did not begin until July 13th.[43]

Meanwhile the work on the station was moving to its conclusion. In the autumn of 1867 Warings were given the contract for erecting the side walls of the train shed, using Gripper's bricks.[44] The foundations for the shed were completed and those for the offices and hotel in front had been begun.[45] Progress on the roof, however, was still slow. Barlow was instructed to make another official complaint to the Butterley Company in November 1867. Under this pressure the Company agreed to build a second scaffold, similar to the first, as a means of expediting the work – the Midland Committee remarking ominously that the cost would be liable to fall on the contractors.[46] A fierce frost ensued in January 1868, and it was not until February that the work got fully into its stride at last. Four ribs were then reported to be complete, with two more under way.[47] The second scaffold was brought into use in March, and thenceforward the work progressed at the rate of three or four ribs a month. The woodwork, slating, and glazing were going ahead in July.[48] The roof was painted brown – though subsequently in about 1876, under strong pressure from Allport (can he have been a man of taste?), the colour was changed to sky-blue with the bases of the trusses painted vermilion.[49]

Warings continued to be dogged to the end by the difficulty of securing an adequate supply of bricks. The last rib of the roof was fitted into place in the middle of September, and it was decided to open the station for traffic on October 1st (ill. 17). It was woefully unfinished. The great screen at the north end was not yet glazed. One of the two scaffolds had been taken down, its timber cut up to form the paving of the platforms. The other was still in use for the erection of the second screen at the south end of the building. A temporary booking-office was in use, which Crossley had been in-

17. *Interior of the completed station.*

structed to provide in June.[50] None of the permanent booking-offices or waiting-rooms had yet been built. Even the buffer-stops were still a matter of discussion between Barlow and Matthew Kirtley, the Midland's Locomotive Engineer.[51] Gilbert Scott had agreed to design a cab-stand. This continued to be the subject of argument until the following February, when at last its erection was agreed upon, at a contract price of £506; the work was still in progress in April.[52] These things could not be waited for. The Company's need to draw a revenue from bringing the line into full operation was paramount. The passengers' comfort would be attended to in due time.

It is not surprising, therefore, that when the first trains began to run in and out of the station, on the appointed October 1st, it was with no inaugural ceremony. The event attracted little notice in the press. When it was mentioned at all, it was the subject of the briefest of paragraphs. The *Illustrated London News*, for example, merely informed its readers vaguely that the station was 'the largest in the world'.[53]

There is irony in all this. The Company had worked so hard, for six years, to secure its own access to London; and when that access had been achieved, instead of proclaiming, with a flourish of trumpets, that it had arrived in the capital, it slipped in almost unobserved. As the Midland clerks moved their stock of tickets and equipment over from King's Cross in the small hours, the Company's entry seemed most to resemble that of a thief in the night.

The morning, however, brought a great innovation with it. If we disregard the only night mail from Leeds and the first down morning train, which followed the pattern of the services from King's Cross, the first new train to leave St Pancras was the ten o'clock express for Manchester, which called at Kentish Town – as almost all trains did at that time, to provide connections from outer London and the City – and ran thence to Leicester without stopping. The distance was 97½ miles, and it was covered in 134 minutes (43.6 mph). This was then the longest non-stop run in the world. There were two such trains in each direction every weekday: a clear indication of the kind of express service the Midland had in mind for the future.

* * * *

For two years after the passing of the Act sanctioning the London extension, the Company had concentrated the whole of its effort on the building of the railway from Bedford and of the train-shed, which was the first necessity for the reception of passengers at St Pancras. It had still to provide for the permanent booking-offices, waiting-rooms, and other amenities that would be required; and for the hotel that was to supply the station's façade on to the Euston Road. When, in May 1865, the Company decided to hold a limited competition for the design of the station buildings and hotel, it invited eleven architects to compete, listing them, not very accurately, as follows:[54]

G H Stokes,[55] Edward Walters,[56] E M Barry,[57] Edward I'Anson,[58].......... Somers,[59] G S Clarke,[60] 'the architect of the passenger station at Exeter',[61] T C Sorby,[62] F P Cockerell,[63] H F Lockwood,[64] and Gilbert Scott. The premiums were fixed in their final form in July: the successful competitor to carry his plans into execution at the usual rates of commission, with three other prizes of £200, £100 and £50.[65]

Not all the architects in the Committee's list in fact competed. Those who did were Walters, Barry, Clarke, Lloyd, Sorby, Cockerell, Lockwood, and Scott. To these were added – presumably by additional invitation – H A Darbishire,[66] T C Hine,[67] and Owen Jones.[68]

In August Barry, Cockerell, and Scott all asked for an extra month for sending in their designs, which was granted.[69] The competitors' work was submitted in the autumn and exhibited in the Shareholders' Room at Derby in December. Early in the New Year it was announced that the Directors had put Scott's designs first (plate I; ills. 21-23). Next, in order of merit, they placed Clarke, Barry, and Sorby.[70]

A good many architectural competitions of this kind were held in the Victorian age, until the strange proceedings in the one for the Law Courts in 1866-74 discredited them.[71] St Pancras station is the only railway building of importance in London that was designed in this way. The Midland Directors did not employ an assessor to guide them in their choice, as municipal bodies did – and this was made a matter of reproach to them later.[72] None of the competitors objected at the time or criticized – directly, at least – Scott's victory. But two of the runners-up had complaints to make. Sorby sent a circular letter to the Directors of the Company, in which he said that 'certain points in detail in the plans sent in by him upon which he had conferred with the General Manager had been communicated by the latter to the other competitors, who had embodied such details in their plans to his, Mr Sorby's detriment'. After questioning Allport on the matter, the Board firmly replied that it considered he had 'acted both honourably and impartially through the whole proceedings'.[73] Somers Clarke felt moved to write a letter to the *Builder* pointing out that Scott had gone far beyond the instructions laid down to the competitors.

> 'It is manifest,' wrote Clarke, 'that the addition of two extra stories of bedrooms to a building of 600 ft. frontage must necessarily give it a vast advantage in dignity and importance of effect over one of less altitude, providing less accommodation.
>
> 'The exact adherence to printed instructions, as a rule, would fetter too much, and probably defeat the intention of getting the best design out of the profession by public boards; still, the extent of accommodation, involving as it does the ultimate cost of a building, is of such primary importance to shareholders in a commercial undertaking, that it ought not to be left to the individual discretion of the competitors themselves, as in this case'.[74]

Clarke's argument is a strong one, and, considering his own position in the matter, most temperately stated. It is heavily reinforced if one looks at the estimates put in by the other competitors. At £316,000 Scott's was over £50,000 higher than the next most expensive design; the lowest, Lockwood's, was under £136,000.[75]

Of the designs by other competitors, only that by Owen Jones has survived (*ill. 18*). He was unusual in making the hotel subsidiary to the station with Barlow's roof placed between two towers and the hotel concentrated on the west side of the site.[76] Other entries concealed the station roof, and F P Cockerell was criticised for creating "a façade, that looks more like the buildings for a new university than a railway terminus."[77] It is easy to guess why the Midland Directors chose Scott's. Putting it at the very lowest, it was a powerful piece of showmanship; and that – for reasons we have already seen – was exactly what the Company required. Nice-minded critics might sneer at it, and did. None of them could deny that it was effective for its purpose: obliterating its rivals, making Euston appear the old-fashioned

18. Owen Jones's competition entry, 1865.

muddle it was and King's Cross a very ordinary piece of austere engineer's building. The Midland Board were business men, making their choice on the broadest commercial grounds. That was their duty to the Company's shareholders, and they performed it faithfully.

They could also feel that in securing the services of Scott they had brought off a coup: for he was the most famous British architect then alive, not least because in 1863 he had won the competition for the design of the Albert Memorial in South Kensington. His work had lain primarily in the building of new churches and the restoration of old ones. But he had also had considerable experience of designing public buildings, from the workhouses that supplied him with bread and butter in the 1830s to the Preston Town Hall, completed in 1862, and the Leeds Infirmary, on which he was still engaged in 1865. He had never designed a commercial building on a big scale, however: nothing larger than Beckett's Bank in Leeds, then in course of erection. It was something of a triumph for the Midland Railway to attract him into a wholly new field.

How characteristic it all is, and how full of irony! Characteristic of the self-confidence of mid-Victorian England, of pride in its achievement and desire to give it tangible expression. Ironic because those Directors, when they deliberately chose the grandest and most expensive of the projects put before them, stood on the edge of a commercial crisis more dangerous – in their line of business at least – than any they had had to meet since the 'forties. Had their decision been delayed only six months, it must inevitably have been different. It is safe to say that in that event the St Pancras station we know would never have been built.

19. George Gilbert Scott, drawing by George Richmond, 1877.

What was it that drew Scott, on his side, into the competition, for a build-ing that lay so far outside his normal practice? He could have any amount of work he pleased. He was one of the first architects to maintain an office on the scale of a factory,[78] and the factory was always in full employment. He tells us himself that he was persuaded to compete, after refusing more than once, by his friend Joseph Lewis, one of the Midland Company's Directors; and that he drew out his designs in September and October 1865 in a small hotel at Hayling, near Portsmouth, where he and his wife were detained by the illness of one of his sons. He goes on to reveal what must surely have been the main reason for his decision: 'Having been disap-pointed, through Lord Palmerston, of my ardent hope of carrying out my style in the Government offices, . . I was glad to be able to erect one build-ing in that style in London.'[79]

Scott is referring to the fierce battle he had been engaged in from 1856 to 1861 over the erection of the new Government offices in Whitehall. There, too, a competition had been held, and after a good deal of curious manoeu-vring Scott had been entrusted with the commission. A change of govern-ment ensued in 1859, which brought Palmerston into power as Prime Minister. He disliked the Gothic style, and in his tough 'no-nonsense' way he insisted that Scott should substitute an Italian one or resign the work to someone else. It was an outrageous demand, and a man of more delicate sensibility than Scott would doubtless have refused to modify his position

20. Elevation of Scott's design for the Foreign Office, 1860-61.

and forced the Government to dismiss him. But he felt that 'to resign would be to give up a sort of property which Providence had placed in the hands of my family' and would merely play the game of those of his fellow-architects who had supported Palmerston.[80] Accordingly he gave way and prepared, entirely against the grain, the Italianate building that now houses the Foreign Office.

That battle had ended four years before Scott entered the competition for St Pancras. But his indignation was undying; and here – we can almost listen in the arguments of his friends, headed by the persuasive Mr Lewis – was a chance to display to London, on a fine open site and in conjunction with a masterpiece of iron engineering, something of the beliefs and the vision that had inspired him in the Whitehall competition of 1856.

It should be quite unnecessary to say that he did not merely re-use for the station the designs that had been rejected for the Government offices.[81] The site was different: level and flat in Whitehall, at St Pancras sloping and raised high above the Euston Road. No vertical scale like that of St Pancras would have been acceptable in Whitehall. The earlier building had been designed in Portland stone throughout,[82] whereas it is of the essence of St Pancras that it is built of brick. But the matter is put quite beyond dispute by the water-colour drawing of Scott's diploma design for the Foreign Office, which is in the Royal Academy *(ill. 20)*. To compare it with St Pancras is to see that the two buildings are both in the Gothic style and both asymmetrical; and that there resemblance ends. We may accept Pevsner's judgement when he writes of this story as a legend and adds: 'all that is true is that he [Scott] had made a thorough study of French and Italian Gothic details for that building [the Foreign Office] and put them to good purpose now'.[83]

21. Scott's competition drawing for the Euston Road elevation, 1865.

It is not very easy to do justice to Scott. Masterful and often insensitive, energetic beyond bounds, monumentally self-complacent – he is at his least likeable in his own writings. But if they are often unattractive, they are of great interest. They show that his art was not by any means merely mechanical, that he thought about some at least of the problems facing architecture in his time: about branches of it, indeed, that concerned him relatively little, like street-fronts in towns and commercial buildings. It is surprising to find him, in the 1850s, giving the warmest praise to the engine-sheds at Camden Town, remarking on the roof of New Street station in Birmingham and on the Gare de l'Est.[84] It is true that in commending those engine-sheds he observes that 'their whole aspect is that of Gothic buildings' and that it is only rarely and with reluctance that he finds anything to admire in classical or Italian architecture. But then he was profoundly and sincerely inspired by the whole Gothic world, which he studied unremittingly for the last thirty years and more of his life. His enthusiasm had the pure flame of passion, kindled by the influence of Pugin, and it is truly engaging. If Scott undertook St Pancras partly for the profit the commission would bring him (and why not?) and partly to get even with Palmerston, he was equally moved by the opportunity it afforded him to erect a building that should exemplify all that he most admired, on a scale bigger than that of any other modern Gothic work in London save the Houses of Parliament. Even to a man so eminent in his profession, it was a great prize. We cannot wonder that, in the end, he decided to compete for

22. Scott's competition drawing for the Pancras Road elevation, 1865.

it: nor – given his special talents and the needs of the Midland Railway at the time – that he should have been adjudged the winner. Having won, he wrote to the Midland Board very handsomely to express his 'high sense of the honour done in accepting his designs, and of the importance of the trust committed to him'.[85]

Scott's plans were accepted, in their definitive form, in April 1866. They involved in one important respect a change in the train-shed, for it had been determined that, in the interests of visitors staying in the hotel, a screen must be provided at the south end of the station, to shut out noise an dirt (*ill. 35*). A screen similar to that provided by Barlow at the north end was therefore added. Scott had been obliged for financial reasons to reduce the scale of the whole, as he had originally conceived it, by omitting two floors

23. T G Jackson's drawing of the ground floor coffee room, 1865.

of station offices and one floor from the hotel.[86] This was the end of the
plan for moving the Company's headquarters to London. The formidable
crisis of that summer put the whole vast and costly scheme out of court for
the present. No more is heard of it until November 21st, when the South
Construction Committee asked Scott to send in 'alternative plans for the St
Pancras station buildings', with an estimate of the cost of each.[87] On
December 5th he attended a meeting of the Midland Board with new plans
and drawings, explaining that these would enable a reduction of £20,000 to
be made in the total cost of the building. His proposals were accepted, and
he was enjoined to make further economies 'wherever it was practicable to
do so'.[88] A fortnight later a clerk of the works was appointed, John Saville,
at a salary of four guineas a week. He entered on his duties on January 1, 1867.[89]

Scott fought hard from the outset to maintain high standards of finish.
He had, for example, decided that he wanted the building to be executed in
Gripper's patent bricks from Nottingham.[90] When tenders came in, they

were found to be expensive, and Scott was persuaded to agree to substitute, at the sides of the building, cheaper bricks supplied by T H Gray of Swannington in Leicestershire. At the end of April, however, Gray declined to provide the bricks since the size required was different from that which he normally made. The end of the matter was that Scott had his way, and Gripper's bricks were used throughout.[91]

From the Company's point of view, none the less, retrenchment of expenditure was now obligatory, and in May it was decided that for the present only that part of the building which was essential for the purposes of the station should be proceeded with. When Scott attended a meeting of the Committee to show the final elevations, he was instructed to 'reduce the cost of decoration and especially to dispense with the use of granite columns wherever he could do so without sacrificing the essential nature of the building'. Work was to be confined to the basement, ground, and first floors east of the main entrance – though including the 'great archway' for that entrance itself. Tenders were to be invited for this part of the work, together with a temporary roof, as well as for the building as a whole.[92] They were not asked for, however, until December. A list of twelve firms was then agreed upon. Nine were London firms, including two whose names are still familiar, Cubitt and Trollope. But a fortnight later, the tenders having come in (with a rapidity incredible to us now), those who had submitted them were all told that the Directors had decided to postpone the execution of the work for at least a year; their tenders had therefore been left for them at Scott's office, unopened.[93]

The whole of the year 1867 had thus gone by without any progress being made towards erecting even a limited part of the hotel. Below, the foundations of the station and hotel buildings were being laid by Warings; above, the iron roof, so long delayed, was beginning to take shape at last; the railway Directors took the plunge. Having persuaded Scott to agree to some further economies in Warings' tender (through replacing oak by deal, some Leicestershire slates by Welsh, Ketton stone by Ancaster, and through a reduction in the ornament)[94] the Board agreed to go ahead. Scott had estimated that Stage I of the building would cost £38,090. Messrs. Jackson & Shaw, one of the firms that had tendered for the work in 1867, secured the contract on March 31st at £37,580.[95]

*   *   *   *

In the relations between architects and their clients, it is a common experience that there should be a honeymoon period at first, when they stimulate one another and find pleasure in their collaboration, followed by a much more difficult phase, in which the client complains that the architect is thwarting his wishes or incurring additional costs unnecessarily, and the architect finds the client ignorant and unreasonable. This was exactly the history of the Midland Company's dealings with Scott. He had shown himself amenable – for a man of his eminent position and autocratic temper, remarkably amenable – in agreeing to economies that impaired, in some small measure, his original design. On their side the Directors of the Company had at first shown themselves deferential, even a shade obsequious, towards their distinguished architect.[96] Now, however, their tone towards him changes.

On July 15, 1868, the work being held up through inadequate deliveries of Gripper's bricks, Scott accepted some from Leicestershire.[97] In November Barlow was reporting delays in the supply of stone and Scott was using a second quarry as well as the one of his first choice.[98] Scott's report to the Committee in December shows him clearly on the defensive. It is no more than a covering letter for two reports from Saville, his 'excellent clerk of works', whose 'zeal and energy' he commends. Saville's tone is at once plaintive and firm: 'Under the circumstances I do not see how it was possible to do much more and ensure good work; there is always a great deal more difficulty in obtaining good work when so much pressure is put on. I have felt extremely anxious they should not advance so rapidly as to abandon all hope and [?in] respect to quality and complete finish by substituting bulk and quantity.'[99]

The booking office seems to have been completed very early in 1869 *(plate III; ills. 24-25)*.[100] Smaller details followed. Scott was asked to prepare designs for the gas-fittings to be used in the station, and on his recommendation F A Skidmore of Coventry – who had executed ironwork for Scott before, notably the Hereford Cathedral screen of 1862 – was commissioned to make them.[101] On the other hand Scott's design for a clock-face was rejected flat in June, 'in consequence of the expense being so great'.[102]

Stage II of the work was now showing above the horizon: the construction and fitting up of the first instalment of the hotel. Scott's estimate for this, including the Clock Tower on the corner of Pancras Road, was £58,715. The work was not put out to tender. Jackson & Shaw were invited to undertake it at the same scale of prices as that of their original contract, and a year later their commission was extended to include the tower over the Great Archway.[103] Where the furnishing and equipment of the hotel was concerned, however, the Committee showed itself less and less willing to give Scott a free hand. He was told that he was to confer with it before he ordered any internal fittings.[104] He was still able to get his own way on some things. He had, for example, been consulting with 'Mr Haden, the eminent warming engineer' about the heating of the station and hotel since 1867,[105] and in

24. *The booking office in its original layout. The entrance from the taxi road is on the left.*

25. *Corbels on the north wall of the booking office. The engine-driver and guard are easily identifiable. Below we have apparently an engineer and a signal boy.*

September 1870 on his proposal, Haden's tender for the heating installation was accepted.[106] Shortly afterwards, however, the Committee told Scott what kind of firegrates it would like to see put in, adding that 'when he is about to procure tenders for grates and mantelpieces . . .[it wished] to have an opportunity of stating the names of some firms who are good customers to the Midland Railway, to be included in the list of those invited to tender'.[107] This request was not by any means unreasonable, and there is nothing to show that Scott resented it. But it was one more sign that the Midland Directors were beginning to exercise a much closer control over his than they had before. It was a foretaste of more serious difficulties to come.

The work on the hotel proceeded at a leisurely pace, and Scott must at times have felt much disheartened. In 1872, however, an unexpected new ally arrived to press for the completion of his great design. In June of the previous year the Board had resolved that steps should be taken to secure a Manager for the hotel 'by advertisement or otherwise'.[108] It proved a long and difficult quest. Three applicants for the post were interviewed by the Committee in February 1872. Evidently none of them pleased, for it was agreed to summon another, Mr R Etzensberger, who had been Manager of the Victoria, one of the chief hotels in Venice, and had undertaken the

26. *The hotel entrance hall, 1876.*

27. *The hotel coffee room, 1876. The original decoration shown here was painted over in 1904, and other Gothic features removed.*

commissariat for the Nile steamers as far as the first cataract.[109] The Committee seems to have recognized that he was a cut above any of the other candidates, for it agreed to the delay that was involved and to the payment of his expenses.[110] When he was offered the post he said he would not be willing to accept it unless the Midland Railway was prepared to complete the hotel more or less as it had originally been planned. It is obvious, from this and from his subsequent transactions with the Company, that Mr Etzensberger was not only at the top of his profession but also a man of impressive personality. By laying down this condition he placed the Committee in a dilemma. It was resolved at a critical meeting on June 4th, when it was decided by nine votes to three to confer with Scott about the completion of the hotel. Among the minority, who resisted undertaking further work on the building, was W E Hutchinson, the former Chairman of the Company, who may well have tired of defending its expenditure on the hotel. The Committee's decision was endorsed by the Board, and in due course by the shareholders in August. In presenting their recommendation, the Directors made it perfectly clear that Etzensberger's pressure upon them had been decisive.[111]

What had now been agreed to was not quite the completion of the whole. Scott had been asked to limit himself for the moment to finishing the entire front and, at the back, two stories only of the curved wing at the west end, the first floor to be covered with a terrace roof.[112] On October 1st the Committee accepted an offer, transmitted through him, from Jackson & Shaw to finish the whole, except for the ironwork, at an advance of 10 per cent on the price they had quoted in their first tender in 1867: a reflection of the sharp rise in the cost of building materials that had appeared in 1871.[113]

On October 1, 1872 the newly-appointed Manager was asked to prepare for opening the first part of the hotel in five months' time.[114] A list of firms who were to be invited to tender for the supply of furniture and plate was drawn up, and he was authorized to lay in a stock of wines and liqueurs, not only from the usual countries of supply but from as far afield as Austria, Hungary and the Levant.[115] In November and December a series of tenders was accepted:[116]

Plate	Elkington	£4,524 12s 9d
Furniture	Gillow	£21,543 (2nd highest tender)
China	Royal Porcelain Co., Worcester	no price given
Glass	P. & C. Osler	____
Beds and bedding	Peyton & Peyton	____
Bed and table linen	Pegler of Leeds	____
Ironmongery	D. & E. Binley	____
Gas-fittings	Skidmore	£3,882
Decoration	Sang[117]	£9,340

28. The ladies' coffee room over the hotel entrance.

Scott worked closely with Gillow's. He was paid 200 guineas for supervising the designs they submitted and himself designed four easy chairs for the coffee room.[118] John Walker, who had made the great public clocks for the station, inside on the south screen and outside on the tower, was invited to supply a series for the private rooms in the hotel, nicely graded in size and price, from £25 each for those with an 8-inch dial for the best sitting-rooms down to £8 each for those to be installed in the 'inferior bedrooms'.[119]

Thus equipped, the Midland Grand Hotel opened its doors to guests on May 5, 1873: at that stage only the part east of the departures arch had been completed *(ill. 32)*. 'The Directors have secured the services of a most efficient *maître d'hôtel*', wrote the *Railway News*, announcing the event. 'The apartments are reported to be magnificent and the charges moderate'.[120] Both reports were true. For an hotel of this class the Midland Company's charges were never extortionate *(see p. 116)*. The magnificence was beyond doubt. Further touches of it were still being added after the opening. In June, for example, Erard's were commissioned to provide ten pianos for the best sitting-rooms. Again they were carefully graded: one grand, four oblique, and five cottage. All alike were to be supplied in walnut cases.[121]

When members of the Architectural Association visited 'the monster hotel' in April 1874, some of them felt that the decorative schemes and furnishing were, at one or two points, excessively rich. 'Some coloured decorations by Mr Sang, in the coffee room and elsewhere, were condemned as being too "loud" . . .Exception was taken to the rather "overdone" toilet services of the best bedrooms, said to have cost 30 guineas per set' *(plates IV-V)*. For the rest, however, the party was full of praise. The furniture was commended, and nearly all the wallpapers; 'the coloured ceiling decorations to some of the best bedrooms executed from Sir Gilbert Scott's own designs' were highly admired.[122]

Perhaps the best account of the hotel is that given by the *Building News* in a special article published shortly after that visit took place, accompanied by a fine engraved plate of the whole façade:

> 'The composition bears evidence of that careful subordination of parts which characterizes Sir G. Gilbert Scott's designs. For example, we find the simple semi-circular massive ground-floor windows, the ornate, trefoiled, traceried, and cusped first-floor windows, and the two upper tiers of less detail as they are removed from the eye, each designed with reference to their position, instead of, as too often seen, the most elaborate multiplicity placed so far above the eye as to be thrown away . . . One want, perhaps, is apparent in the façade, taken as a whole, namely a greater connection either by vertical or horizontal lines between the windows, and a want of breadth in some parts . . .

'The ground floor east of the departure gateway consists of entrance hall, staircase, and rooms devoted to the general management, as manager's and clerks' offices, lifts, baggage-rooms, etc., also to refreshment and dining rooms, and necessary offices; a suite of rooms for private letting is also provided. The east end of the arrival gateway has four large rooms set apart for station purposes. A basement extends under this portion of the hotel, and let to Messrs Travers & Sons, wine merchants. The west wing embraces the general public entrance. . . with a covered carriage-way under an arcade leading to a spacious vestibule 54 feet by 22 feet; the coffee room, a fine apartment, with circular ends, occupying the curved part of a wing; the grand staircase, a feature of considerable merit; also lifts, etc.; and the rear of this wing is appropriated to casual visitors, and comprises billiard and smoking rooms, lavatories, and other offices. At the extreme rear of this part are the laundry, drying-rooms, with wash-houses and engine-room below. In the basement under the west wing is the kitchen, and other servants' offices. The first floor is devoted to sitting and bed rooms; the chief feature is a ladies' reading room and dining room, over the entrance. In the rear are billiard rooms, etc.; in all, 52 rooms on this floor. The second, third, and fourth floors are available for letting purposes, in sitting and bedrooms, with all necessary adjuncts. They each contain about 73 rooms, and the whole available area of floors contains about 500 rooms, besides lifts, bathrooms, etc.'[123]

The Company grew alarmed at the size of the bills for all this grand furniture and equipment. In August the Secretary was instructed to write to Scott to point out that a number of the estimates had been exceeded and to insist that no further expenditure should be incurred beyond the existing contracts without the specific assent of the South Construction Committee.[124] Scott was employing his son John Oldrid Scott to supervise the decoration of the west wing, which was still under construction; and when John Oldrid asked that Clayton & Bell (a firm remembered today chiefly for their stained glass) should be instructed to begin detailed studies for the work, his request was turned down flat and he was told that the Company would appoint its own decorator, who would act directly under its orders.[125] The elder Scott evidently took this rebuff hard. He reopened the question with the Committee in January 1874, and again a year later; but the Committee stood firm, handing over the whole decoration of the west wing to Gillow's, a commercial firm that would evidently be more amenable to its control.[126] Though Sang had performed well on the decoration of the east wing, as an associate of Scott's he fell victim to the committee's mistrust of their architect.

75

29. *The music room on the first floor.*

30. *A private sitting room on the first floor.*

This was not the worst, however. In January 1874 there was a dispute between Scott and the Committee about closing the accounts for the first stage of the building, the Committee resolving 'that Mr Scott be informed that his reply on the subject is unsatisfactory'; and at the same meeting, when he submitted plans for the ventilation of the hotel he was told that 'as this Committee have not invited any such specifications and drawings' they were to be returned to him.[127]

Scott was a formidable man, at the summit of his profession. He can have been little accustomed to such peremptory treatment by his clients. He accepted it with patience; and when he went on to explain – as no doubt he ought to have done earlier – the need for the ventilation and for the scheme he proposed, the Committee accepted his plan.[128] This seems to have ended disagreement for the time being, though it came to the surface again when he tried to persuade the Committee to allow the niches on the façade to be filled with the sculptured figures they were intended to hold. The Clerk of Works pointed out that the topmost one on the gable of the west tower facing the Euston Road could be hoisted into place very easily while the builders' scaffolding was still there; but the Committee refused to sanction the expenditure of £100 required for the sculpture and remained adamant in declining to incur any such expenditure afterwards.[129] The result today is that the statue of Britannia, facing out from beside the clock tower eastward over King's Cross, is the only sculptured figure on the building.

There was constant trouble, too, with Scott's *protégé* Skidmore. His delays were complained of in November 1873. Two months later he had to be summoned to a meeting of the South Construction Committee and told of its 'dissatisfaction at the slow manner in which his contract was being proceeded with'. In November 1874 he was called on to complete the gas fittings in the finished part of the hotel immediately. Early in 1876 Etzenberger complained of him to the Committee, and it was decided that his appliances should be set up by the Company's own men, there being no specific contract with Skidmore for fitting.[130]

The furnishing of the hotel, entrusted to Gillow's throughout, reflected the hierarchy of uses on the different floors. Though none of the original furniture survives in the building, we know from the ledger of bills for fitting out the hotel, plus early photographs, that the furniture was mostly of oak or walnut on the ground and first floors, oak or teak on the second, mahogany on the third and ash on the fourth floor *(ills. 26-31)*. The servants on the fifth floor had to be content with 'deal japanned as oak'. Carpets in the public areas of the first and second floors were Axminster, but Brussels with linoleum edging on the third and fourth: on the fifth floor there was simply cocoa matting.[131]

Very little is recorded about the domestic quarters of the hotel, or its

31. *The Oriel Room on the first floor beneath the clock tower.*

kitchen equipment. The servants' accommodation was, of course, planned to be in the top attics, 'the male and female departments having no communication with each other, and approached by different staircases'.[132] What strikes one today, on seeing these top floors, is their enormous scale: on the sixth floor, at the narrowest part of the building, the central corridor is still a dozen feet wide.

At no other time in his long, prolific career did Scott have to consider on any large scale the provision of kitchens, and the accommodation necessarily associated with them in a building of this sort. Accordingly he put himself into the hands of experts who had been concerned with similar work at other large hotels. The planning of the larders followed that at the Charing Cross Hotel, which also gave him the idea of providing a 'gallery' at one side of the kitchen, in which the cooks were to have their meals.[133] The vegetables, we are told, were 'cooked by steam in iron steam-chests (fortunately guarded with safety-valves)'. In the laundry a washing machine, 6 feet in diameter, boiled up to 3,000 pieces of linen daily, after which they were passed through a centrifugal wringer and through drying closets to 'two steam mangling machines' and so to the airing room.[134] The kitchen and the laundry equipment were supplied by Jeakes & Co. of Great Russell Street.[135]

Hydraulically-operated lifts were installed: a fairly new invention, from America. Passengers could not be entrusted to a lift without a safety device. The earliest effective one had been installed, for the first time in regular service, in a New York store by Elisha Otis in 1857.[136] In the St Pancras hotel there were separate lifts for passengers and for luggage, together with others (worked by hand) for food and for coal.[137] Sir William Armstrong supplied the mechanically-operated lifts at a contract price of £710 for the passenger lift, which carried ten people, and £340 for the luggage lift, capable of being loaded to 8cwt.[138] On June 30, 1874 the passenger lift met with an accident (apparently no one was injured). Armstrong accepted liability for the consequential expense and also agreed to build another passenger lift in the west wing on the piston principle, recommended by the engineer Crossley and S W Johnson, the Midland Company's Locomotive Superintendent.[139] New lifts supplied by the American Elevator Company were installed in 1891.

As the west wing of the hotel approached completion in 1875, additional contracts were placed for the furniture and equipment required, generally with the same firms as before.[140] There is some uncertainty about the date when the work was at last finished and the entire hotel brought into use. On July 4, 1876 the South Construction Committee resolved that the whole building should be handed over to the Way and Works Committee with effect from July 1st.[141] That would seem decisive if it were not that another identical resolution was passed by the same Committee on April 3, 1877.[142] Scott's final accounts were settled on September 5, 1876.[143] In the winter after Scott was paid off, the finishing touches were made to the Grand Staircase. Special scaffolding was erected for the decoration of the ribbed vault spandrels, which used figural cartoons of the virtues supplied by another prominent Gothicist, E W Godwin. He had designed the figures for a castle in County Limerick, and when damp prevented their execution in that building, it was an easy matter to rework them for the Midland Grand, with the addition of the railway's coat-of-arms. Their moralising medievalism was perfectly suited to this architectural setting *(plates VI-VII)*.[144]

The final costs were disclosed by the Chairman to the shareholders in February 1877. The fabric, he told them, had cost £304,335; decoration and fittings, £49,000; furnishing, £84,000. The total expenditure on the hotel was thus £438,000.[145]

We have no similar statement of the final costs of the station proper. The aggregate price of the two contracts into which it was divided was £436,000.[146] Allowing for fees (not included in this last figure), for an increase over the contract price in respect of the roof, and for miscellaneous additional payments – as, for example, for Scott's cab-shelter and for the

32. The Ordnance Survey of 1874, showing St Pancras and King's Cross stations. At this stage the west wing of the hotel had not been built.

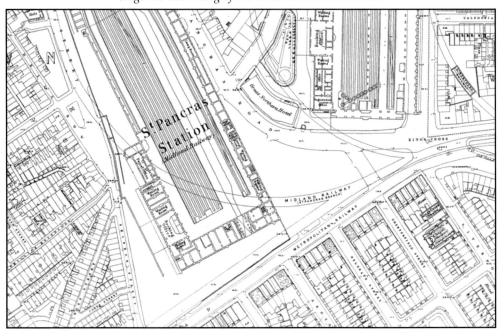

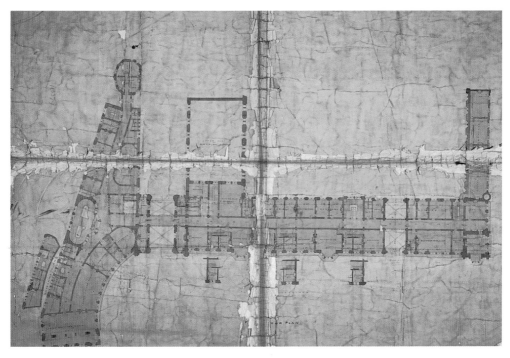

Plate I. Scott's plan of the first floor of the hotel, 1866.

Plate II. Building St Pancras station, as depicted by C J Richardson in 1871. The huddle of buildings in Weston Place, Pancras Road was soon to be demolished.

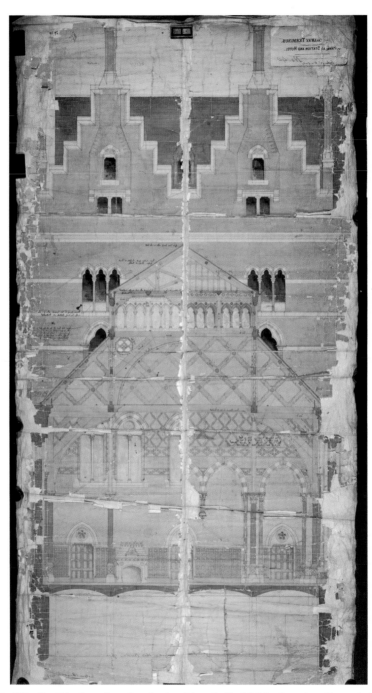

Plate III. Scott's drawing for the booking hall, 1866, showing the original hipped roof and lantern.

Plate IV. F Sang's design for the Ladies' Reading Room ceiling, 1873.

Plate V. F. Sang's design for a temporary coffee room ceiling, 1873.

Plate VI. The main staircase of the hotel showing the painted decoration in the vault by E W Godwin.

Plate VII. Patience. One of E W Godwin's depictions of the virtues.

Plate VIII. Gilded archway in the entrance hall.

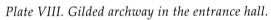

Plate IX. John O'Connor's famous painting of St Pancras at sunset, 1884, looking down from Pentonville.

Plate X. Victoria Railway Terminus, Bombay, 1878.

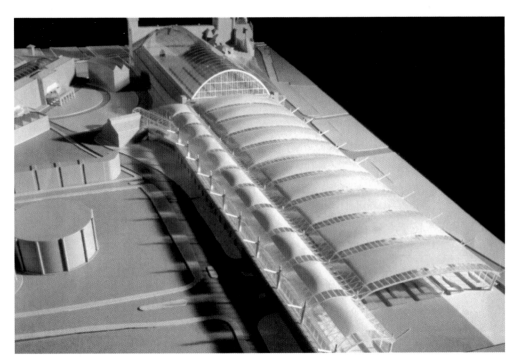

Plate XI. Design by Nick Derbyshire for the International Terminus at St Pancras.

Plate XII. Dismantling the gasholders, 2002. These guide frames date from1880.

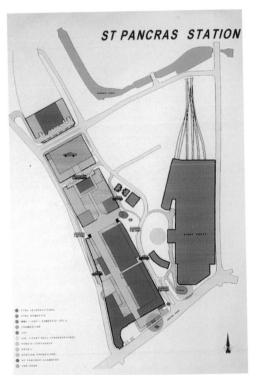
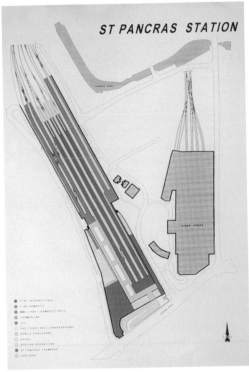

Plate XIII. Plans of the International Terminus. Left: Concourse (street) level.
Right: Rail (platform) level.

Plate XIV. Perspective of interior of the trainshed after completion of CTRL works.

clocks – it can be said with confidence that St Pancras passenger station cost the shareholders of the Midland Company not much less than a million pounds.

* * * *

One further addition had yet to be made to the complex of buildings on the site. The goods traffic of the Midland Company continued to expand until it outgrew the station built for it on the north side of Agar Town – commodious though that was by the standards of the 1860s. Its warehouse contained 90,000 square feet. Before it had been open a year it had been necessary to double the size; and Allport was then predicting that a further enlargement would be required by 1870.[147] The financial troubles of the later 'sixties no doubt deferred it. By 1874, however, the provision had become inescapably necessary, and the Company began to seek powers to acquire fourteen more acres of Somers Town, to the west of the passenger station. An outcry then arose. The Home Secretary's attention was drawn to the scheme and to the Midland Company's omission to provide for reconstruction or even to supply a return of the number of families that would be affected. The proposals were deleted from the Bill.[148] The Company got the powers it sought in the following year, at the price of certain concessions. The Metropolitan Board of Works succeeded in forcing it to set back the front of the proposed goods station on to the Euston Road, to permit that road to be widened to 70 feet, and it also agreed to widen Skinner Street and Ossulston Street, which bounded the area it was occupying on its east and west sides. The Company was, moreover, required to sell land for the erection of dwellings for those displaced by the new development, in Hampden Street and Ossulston Street.[149]

These powers secured, the Midland set about buying up all the property it needed,[150] and in February 1876 it decided to enter into an agreement with the Metropolitan Artizans Dwelling Company for the building of the working-class houses.[151] The project went ahead, however, very slowly, and caused much more fierce feeling before it was completed. More than 10,000 people were to be displaced, and when the work got under way in earnest, early in 1878, they complained vociferously that the Company was not complying with the provisions of its Act of 1875. *The Builder*, investigating the matter, found it hard to say where right might lie, but it observed that 'a visit to the spot would be sufficient to convince the most sceptical that a more dilapidated or disease-ridden block of hovels does not exist in any part of the metropolis'.[152] A year later, though the process continued without pause, the future use of the site was a matter of guesswork. Was it really to be a goods station after all? Or a wholesale vegetable market

33. Somers Town Goods Depot, exterior view.

34. Somers Town Goods Depot, interior view.

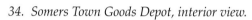

instead? Or 'a garden and recreation ground for the use of the visitors patronizing the St Pancras hotel'?[153]

The indignation of those who had been displaced must have grown greater as years went by and no new building appeared. It was not until 1883 that at length the work of constructing the goods station began, to the designs of the Company's Engineer for New Works, John Underwood. The contractor was the reliable Firbank (ills. 33-34).[154]

The work started off with the erection of a wall three-quarters of a mile long round the whole site: a superb piece of brickwork, faced with Leicester-shire bricks of an unusually small size, with Staffordshire blue bricks on the inside. They were set throughout in cement, no lime being used anywhere in the whole work. The delicacy of the pointing and the evenness of the bricklaying were a much admired achievement.

Inside, the station was built on two storeys, the upper connected directly to the main line immediately north of the Pancras Road bridge, the lower being reached by means of hydraulic lifts similar to those employed to furnish access to the vault under the passenger station. This ground-level station provided, among other thins, a much-needed addition to the facili-ties available for handling coal. There were already two depots to the north of the passenger station, one on each side of the line. This supplied a third. It must have seemed then that the expansion of the Company's coal trade was illimitable. There was also special provision for potato and vegetable merchants, taking advantage of the proximity of St Pancras to Covent Garden Market.

The main front of the station, on to the Euston Road, was decoratively treated, but the ornament was – appropriately – sober in comparison with Scott's. The arches of the doors and open arcade were turned in brick and Mansfield stone, and they were filled with a series of delicate grilles of ham-mered iron by John Potter of South Molton Street. The remainder of the ironwork was by Gimson's of Leicester.

Almost none of this now survives. With the decline of railway freight traffic, the Somers Town Goods Depot was taken out of use, and in 1975 its site was earmarked by the government as the location for the new British Library. Work began on the first phase of the library building in 1984 to the designs of Colin St John Wilson and Partners. Like the Goods Depot, the library is an extraordinarily complex engineering structure with up to five levels of basement packed full of books on rolling stacks. And just as the Midland Railway had been attacked for the manner in which the site was cleared, so a hundred years later the library project was sniped at from all sides – for its design, its cost (ultimately £511 million), and for the time it took to complete. Regardless of whether it is a suitable architectural neighbour to Scott's masterpiece, it is a wonderful use to have alongside the station, adding scholarly dignity to the Euston Road.

[1] To be strictly correct, it used the title 'Southern Construction Committee' from May 11 to September 5, 1864. Its minutes are in PRO RAIL 491/280-83. The Committee remained in being long after the line was completed; but after 1882 its minutes were merged with those of the General Purposes Committee.

[2] The contracts are listed in Barnes, 209. A separate contract was made with John Knowles of Shefford for the building of the Ampthill Tunnel (716 yards long).

[3] PRO RAIL 491/280, min. 239.

[4] *Ibid.*, min. 245

[5] *Ibid.*, mins. 307, 314; Barnes, 210-11.

[6] PRO RAIL 491/280, mins 239, 252.

[7] Barnes, 222-3.

[8] PRO RAIL 491/280, min. 381.

[9] PRO RAIL 491/411 (Waring), 3/43 (Butterley).

[10] A Clifton-Taylor, *The Pattern of English Building* (1962), 145.

[11] Here is an exception to the general rule stated by Mr Clifton-Taylor that 'since the end of the eighteenth century it has for some reason never been the practice to lay Welsh slates in courses of diminishing size, as with all other natural slates' (*ibid.* 172). The practice adopted at St Pancras, of using slates of four different sizes, was a compromise between uniformity and steady gradation, in which each course differs slightly in size from its successor. The Swithland slates on the roof of the hotel were laid in the traditional manner, as can still be seen today.

[12] A detailed narrative of the work, based on the Midland Company's records, is given in Barnes, chaps. 10-12. It is most regrettable, however, that Mr Barnes seldom gives any specific references to the sources of his information.

[13] PRO RAIL 491/280, min. 80.

[14] *Ibid.*, min. 308.

[15] PRO RAIL 491/280, min. 364.

[16] W E Brown, *St Pancras Open Spaces and Disused Burial Grounds* (1911), 7-9.

[17] *Builder* 19 May 1866, 374.

[18] *Builder* 7 Sept 1867, 656.

[19] Florence E Hardy, *The Life of Thomas Hardy* (1933), i. 58-9. Mrs Hardy assigns the episode to 'probably the year 1865 or thereabouts' instead of 1866. For Hardy's architectural career, see the introduction by C J P Beatty to *The Architectural Notebook of Thomas Hardy* (Dorchester, 1966).

[20] *St Pancras Past and Present* (1874), 62.

[21] Cf. The vituperative introduction to [R P Prosser] *A Plea for St Pancras Churchyard* [1874]: British Library, 10351 dd. 9(15).

[22] H B Wheatley, *London Past and Present* (1891), iii. 22.

[23] PRO RAIL 491/280, min. 511.

[24] *The Times*, 11 April 1866, 10; 12 April 1866, 6.

[25] *Annual Register*, 1866, Part I, 184.

[26] Sir J Clapham, *Economic History of Modern Britain* (1926-38), ii. 375-6.

[27] F. McDermott, *The Life and Work of Joseph Firbank* (1887), 54-5.

[28] PRO RAIL 491/280, min.418.

[29] *Ibid.*, min.511.

[30] *Ibid.*, min.469.

[31] Cf. For example, *ibid.*, min 485 (February 5, 1867) and 568 (July 17, 1867).

[32] *Ibid.*, min. 397.

[33] *Ibid.*, min. 542; PRO RAIL 491/281, min. 644.

[34] PRO RAIL 491/280, min. 573; PRO RAIL 491/281, min. 633.

[35] PRO RAIL 491/281, min. 644. For details of this scaffold see the account by its designer, Sir J G N Alleyne: *Papers read at the Royal Institute of British Architects*, 1872, 71-9.

[36] There may have been more to be said in defence of the Butterley Company; but since it has destroyed all its documentary records of this period, we shall never know.

[37] British Library, 8235 bb. 75 (11).

[38] This was only just true. The dividend for 1860 was $6^3/_4$ per cent – the highest since the days of Hudson, under whom dividends were freely supplemented out of capital; that for 1866 – a year of crisis – was 6 $^1/_8$ per cent. The half-yearly declaration in June 1867 was at the rate of $2^3/_4$ per cent, which was higher than the corresponding dividend for 1859. In the end $5^1/_2$ per cent was paid in all, even in 1867, and this climbed steadily up to $7^1/_4$ per cent in 1872.

[39] British Library, 8235 bb. 77 (3).

[40] The report of this committee is in PRO RAIL 1110/329 (with the 48th half-yearly report of the Company, February 19, 1868). Professor Checkland, in his *Rise of Industrial Society in England* (1964), 44, lists the Midland among the railway companies whose affairs were 'publicly inquired into, and found to have been mismanaged', at this time. The nearest thing to any such inquiry was this one; and it was not public, nor did it conclude that there had been mismanagement. Baines's final words, when the Committee was wound up is February 1869, were quite explicit: 'We have not been able to detect any one single thing in their [the Directors'] conduct of our business which we could have wished to see otherwise' (PRO RAIL 491/9, 50th half-yearly meeting, p.10).

[41] PRO RAIL 491/281, mins. 649, 656.

[42] *Ibid.*, min. 716.

[43] For the terms of the agreement between the two companies respecting the use of the Metropolitan line see Barnes, 245.

[44] PRO RAIL 491/281, mins. 620, 640, 659. For Gripper see p.64 below.

[45] *Ibid.*, min. 673.

[46] *Ibid.*, mins. 679, 689.

[47] *Ibid.*, min. 713.

[48] *Ibid.*, min. 841.

[49] M.P.I.C.E. 30 (1869-70), 95, 105; Williams, 345; paint analysis by Catherine Hassall for Rail Link Engineering.

[50] PRO RAIL 491/281, min. 797.

[51] *Ibid.*, min. 905.

[52] *Ibid.*, min. 904, 997, 1111, 1144.

[53] *Illustrated London News*, 3 October 1868, 311.

[54] PRO RAIL 491/280, min. 101.

[55] Principally distinguished as the collaborator with his father-in-law Joseph Paxton in a number of such works as Lismore Castle: H.-R. Hitchcock, *Early Victorian Architecture* (1954), 240-1.

[56] In practice in Manchester, where he designed a number of magnificent warehouses. He is said to have been responsible for the stations on the Midland's Manchester line north of Ambergate (ibid., 387), though 'Ambergate' should probably read 'Rowsley'.

[57] Cf. p.32

⁵⁸ Edward I'Anson III (1812-88). 'Perhaps the ablest London commercial architect from the early 'forties down to the 'seventies': Hitchcock, 375.

⁵⁹ No architect of this name is known. Surely a confusion with Somers Clarke, whose name follows?

⁶⁰ G. Somers Clarke (1825—82), architect of Wanstead Hospital (1861). Engaged at the time on the Auction Mart (now the Overseas Bankers' Club) in Lothbury – 'the most impressive neo-Venetian in London . . . an amazing building for its date': N. Pevsner, *The Buildings of England: the Cities of London and Westminster* (2nd ed., 1962), 100, 239.

⁶¹ This was St David's station, and the architect was Henry Lloyd of Bristol: *Builder*, 18 June 1864, 452.

⁶² Emigrated to Canada in 1883, where he designed hotels and stations for the Canadian Pacific Railway.

⁶³ Second son of C R Cockerell. His chief public work in London was the Freemasons' Hall in Great Queen Street.

⁶⁴ Collaborator with W and R Mawson in some of the most distinguished buildings in Bradford and in the whole development of Saltaire.

⁶⁵ PRO RAIL 491/280, min. 158.

⁶⁶ 'A sort of Gilbert Scott, or more accurately an Alfred Waterhouse, of Victorian housing': Hitchcock, 473.

⁶⁷ Of Nottingham; architect of the Corn Exchange and London Road railway station in that town.

⁶⁸ Closely associated with Paxton on both the first and the second Crystal Palaces. The final list of competitors appears in *Builder*, 13 January 1866, 33, corroborated in *Building News*, 12 January 1866, 30.

⁶⁹ PRO RAIL 491/280, min. 177.

⁷⁰ *Builder*, 16 December 1865, 896; 13 January 1866, 33.

⁷¹ For the Law Courts competition see M H Port, 'The New Law Courts Competition, 1866-67', in *Architectural History* 2 (1968); David Brownlee, *The Law Courts. The Architecture of George Edmund Street* (1984).

⁷² Cf. Pp. pp 111-12

⁷³ PRO RAIL 491/20, min. 6912.

⁷⁴ *Builder*, 10 February 1866, 105.

⁷⁵ The exact estimates were as follows: Scott, £316,000; Hine & Evans, £255,000; Sorby, £245,000; Barry, £236,487; Walters & Barker, £190,000; Jones, £187,000; Clarke, £164,500; Cockerell, £155,000; Lloyd, £150,000; Lockwood & Mawson, £135,792; Darbishire, no estimate. *Ibid.*, 68.

⁷⁶ *Builder*, 16 December 1865, 896.

⁷⁷ *Builder*, 5 May 1866, 318.

⁷⁸ Cf. *Recollections of Thomas Graham Jackson* (Oxford, 1950), 58-9.

⁷⁹ Sir Gilbert Scott, *Personal and Professional Recollections* (1879), 271-2; David B. Brownlee, 'That "Regular Mongrel Affair": G G Scott's Design for the Government Offices', *Architectural History* 28 (1985), 159-82.

⁸⁰ *Ibid.*, 191-2.

⁸¹ The origin of the myth is to be found in *Builder*, 12 May 1866, 340.

⁸² G G Scott, *Explanatory Remarks on the Designs for the new Foreign Office* (n.d.), 8.

⁸³ N Pevsner, *The Buildings of England: London except the Cities of London and Westminster* (1952), 368-9.

⁸⁴ G G Scott, *Remarks on Secular and Domestic Architecture* (1857), 218-9.

⁸⁵ PRO RAIL 491/20, min. 6914.

[86] *Ibid.,* min 6987.

[87] PRO RAIL 491/280, min. 434.

[88] PRO RAIL 491/20, min. 7157.

[89] PRO RAIL 491/280, min.453.

[90] Edward Gripper was an Essex farmer who moved to Nottingham in the 1850s and established a Patent Brick Company at Mapperley in 1867. It was a large concern. He became a prominent citizen of Nottingham, and Mayor in 1880. The patent was not his own. He had negotiated for 'the exclusive local use of Hoffman's continuous burning kilns, whereby the surplus heat after burning passed on to the next chamber so that the kiln never went out' (R Mellors, *Men of Nottingham and Nottinghamshire,* 1924, 232; *Nottingham Daily Guardian,* December 24, 1894). I owe these references to the kindness of Mr K S S Train.

[91] PRO RAIL 491/280, mins. 451, 499, 538, 547. The difference between Gripper's tender and Gray's is worth noting (min. 499). Gripper's prices varied according to the season of delivery. In winter (November-April) they were, for best fronts 50s a thousand, for cappers 37s 6d, for commons 26s 6d; in summer 47s 6d, 36s, and 25s, respectively. Gray quoted 36s for best, 21s for commons, all the year round.

[92] *Ibid.,* min. 546.

[93] PRO RAIL 491/281, mins. 660, 676.

[94] PRO RAIL 491/281, min. 678.

[95] *Ibid.,* min. 753. Jackson & Straw also built many city offices, including Mansion House Buildings in Poultry, and the extensions to Burlington House Piccadilly.

[96] They had engaged him without any understanding about his fees. He asked for £4,000 as an instalment on them in December 1867, and this was agreed. He then stated his charges at 5 per cent on the outlay; if parts of the building only were carried out, he required 2° per cent on the whole for drawings and 2½ per cent on the parts actually constructed. *Ibid.,* mins. 659a, 677.

[97] *Ibid.,* min. 840.

[98] *Ibid.,* min. 931.

[99] PRO RAIL 491/281, min. 963.

[100] *Ibid.,* Saville's second report.

[101] *Ibid.,* mins. 1146, 1168.

[102] *Ibid.,* min. 1181.

[103] *Ibid.,* mins. 1188, 1204, 1210, 1215, 1300.

[104] *Ibid.,* min. 1222.

[105] PRO RAIL 491/280, min 504. Haden's firm is still well known in the business today.

[106] PRO RAIL 491/281. Min 1299.

[107] *Ibid.,* min.1319.

[108] MID 1/20, min. 8707.

[109] Williams, *The Midland Railway,* 351. The Victoria is commended in Murray's *Handbook for Northern Italy* (11th ed., 1869), 370.

[110] PRO RAIL 491/281, min. 1396.

[111] PRO RAIL 491/282, min. 1417; *Railway Times* 36 (1872), 858.

[112] PRO RAIL 491/282, mins. 1421, 1423.

[113] The astonishing proportions of this rise – by nearly 30 per cent – are shown in the tables in K. Maiwald, 'An Index of Building Costs in the United Kingdom, 1845-1938': *Economic History Review,* 2nd ser. 7 (1954-55), 192-3.

[114] PRO RAIL 491/282, min. 1439.

[115] *Ibid.,* mins. 1444, 1446.

[116] *Ibid.,* mins. 1449, 1452-4, 1457-8, 1462-4.

[117] The German-born decorator Frederick Sang, who had been responsible for the interior decoration of Bunning's Coal Exchange and for work at several clubs, e.g. the Travellers' and the Conservative. His St Pancras tender excluded the ground floor, cellars and domestic offices.

[118] PRO RAIL 491/282, mins. 1449, 1474.

[119] *Ibid.,* min. 1461.

[120] *Railway News* 19 (1873), 661.

[121] PRO RAIL 491/282, min. 1496.

[122] *Building News,* 17 August 1874, 437.

[123] *Building News,* 22 May 1874, 554, 558-9.

[124] PRO RAIL 491/282, min 1511.

[125] PRO RAIL 491/282, mins. 1535-6, 1544-5.

[126] *Ibid.,* mins. 1629, 1650, 1747, 1774, 1781, 1812, 1826.

[127] *Ibid.,* mins. 1602-3.

[128] *Ibid.,* mins. 1613, 1632.

[129] *Ibid.,* mins. 1806, 1838, 1843.

[130] PRO RAIL 491/282, mins. 1548, 1620, 1760, 1958.

[131] National Railway Museum, York. *Midland Grand Hotel London, inventory of furniture, fittings, etc.*

[132] *Engineer,* 14 June 1867, 538.

[133] Ibid.

[134] Williams, *The Midland Railway,* 350.

[135] *Building News,* 22 May 1874, 554.

[136] C. Singer *et al., A History of Technology* (Oxford, 1954-8), v. 478. The Westminster Palace Hotel had been provided with lifts in 1860.

[137] In the description in the *Engineer* a distinction is made between the 'ascending chamber' for passengers and the 'lifts' for other purposes. Was 'lift' still a vulgarism?

[138] PRO RAIL 491/282, min. 1502a.

[139] PRO RAIL 491/282, mins. 1718, 1732, 1738.

[140] *Ibid.,* mins. 1891-94, 1903-4.

[141] *Ibid.,* min. 2009.

[142] PRO RAIL 491/283, min. 2960.

[143] *Ibid.,* min. 2024.

[144] Susan Weber Soros, 'E W Godwin and Interior Design' in: Soros, *E W Godwin: Aesthetic Movement Architect and Designer* (1999), 304-5.

[145] PRO RAIL 491/9: 66th half-yearly meeting, February 20, 1877, p.6.

[146] See p. 44

[147] M.P.I.C.E. 25 (1865-66), 285.

[148] *Building News,* 24 April 1874, 445; see also P.P.1874, lix, Cmnd 246.

[149] *Builder,* 15 May 1875, 435-6.

[150] PRO RAIL 491/282, min. 1863.

[151] *Ibid.,* min. 1959.

[152] *Builder,* 30 March 1878, 320.

[153] *Ibid.,* 24 May 1879, 582.

[154] The account that follows is based on McDermott, *Joseph Firbank,* 127-32, *The Times,* 2 November, 1887, 6 and *The Engineer,* 6 April 1888, 272-4, 276.

CHAPTER IV

The Station at Work

We have now considered how the complex of buildings at St Pancras was planned and constructed. It is time to look at the business transacted in them, to see how they have worked in practice over the past hundred years or more.

When the usual teething troubles were past, the passenger trains into and out of the station settled down into a well-defined pattern. From 1868 to 1880 there were two main-line services. Both ran through Bedford and Leicester to Trent, where they divided, one running on through Matlock to Manchester and Liverpool, the other going due north through Chesterfield to Leeds and Bradford. On May 1, 1876, the second of these services was extended to Scotland, through the opening of the Settle & Carlisle line to link up with the Glasgow & South Western system and North British, providing access to Edinburgh. St Pancras thus became the starting-point for a third main line to Scotland, competing with the long-established West Coast and East Coast routes. Both to Edinburgh and to Glasgow its lines were longer, and very much harder to work, owing to their gradients and curves. If the Midland Company and its associates were genuinely to compete, they could not realistically expect to do so by offering a service to the same times as those of their rivals. They could manage it only by providing superior facilities. By 1876, in some respects at least, they had them.

In 1872 the Midland had opened all its trains, without exception, to third-class passengers. No other main-line company had done such a thing before.[1] This was a critically important decision: a bold stroke, both of policy and of business, due primarily to James Allport. It reflected that self-confident energy, tough and adventurous, which is exemplified by the Midland Board throughout these years, with its physical embodiment in the grand station itself. It carried through to a conclusion the ideas that lay behind Gladstone's Act of 1844, which had first given the third-class passenger decent minimum rights. Like that Act, this decision by the Midland Company was bitterly unpopular with those whom it threatened, or seemed

35. *The interior of the station, June 1876, showing the screen erected to protect the hotel bedrooms from the noise and dirt of the station.*

36. *The interior of the station looking north, June 1876. Before the building of platforms 3 and 4, the lines between platforms 5 and 2 were used for storing carriages.*

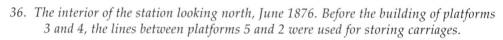

to threaten. The old giants of the railway world, the London & North Western and Great Western Companies, were seriously displeased, and said so; but they were obliged before long to follow suit. By the 'eighties there were few trains in Britain, save on the obdurate railways of Kent and Sussex, from which the third-class passenger was excluded: whereas on the Continent, with rare exceptions – the State Railways in France, the Dutch Rhenish Company, the Danish railways and some of those in North Germany – the older practice continued to prevail.[2] This important discrimination between classes prevails there widely still.[3]

Just over two years later, in October 1874, the Midland exploded another bombshell. It announced that from the beginning of 1875 it would cease to provide second-class accommodation altogether, and that its first-class fares would be reduced to the old second-class rates. Not long afterwards it went a stage further still, undertaking to upholster the seats of all its third-class carriages. Up to that time they had almost universally comprised bare boards – as they did on many Continental railways down to the 1930s.

Again the Midland's rivals were furious; and in these matters they did not all follow the Midland's lead. But whether they did or not, the consequence was plain: that third-class passengers were better off on a Midland train than they were likely to be on any other.

The Midland did not make the mistake of showering benefits on the third-class passenger alone. At the same time it introduced Pullman cars to this country. Preliminary runs, to demonstrate this new American luxury to the Company's directors and officials and to the press, were made from Derby to St Pancras and from St Pancras to Bedford and back in March 1874. Lunch was served on the way (previously prepared, not cooked on board), and these were the first meals ever given to passengers on British trains. The cars went into regular service on June 1st, running up from Bradford to reach St Pancras at 2.5 p.m. and returning at midnight; they were convertible, in the American manner, to provide sleeping accommodation (at a supplementary fee of 6s), and passengers could occupy berths in them from ten o'clock onwards.[4] It was noticed that these cars, running on bogies, achieved a standard of smooth running hitherto unknown in Britain. 'The visitors to Bedford were asked to write their names in a book', wrote a journalist, deeply impressed, 'and they did so without the smallest difficulty when the train was running at the rate of 50 miles an hour.'[5]

When the Settle & Carlisle line was opened, Pullman parlour and sleeping cars were run for first-class passengers in the trains between St Pancras, Edinburgh, and Glasgow. The trains also included splendid twelve-wheeled coaches, 54 ft long, built specially for them, which rode immeasurably better at speed than those of the Midland's competitors. The London & North

Western was unable to use any vehicle more than 33ft long owing to a short traverser at Euston, which was in service until 1882; the Great Northern clung to its horrible vehicles with six wheels (which E L Ahrons suspected were octagonal), running them much later than that in the fastest trains in the world.[6] The Midland could justifiably claim that, if its Scotch expresses took a little longer over their journey than those from Euston or King's Cross, they offered greater comfort to those who used them, rich and poor alike.

It fought just as keenly for other traffic, on less unfavourable terms. In 1880 it opened a new line from Kettering to Nottingham, through Melton Mowbray, which enabled an entirely re-cast service to be introduced from St Pancras to Leeds and Bradford. The new trains were always knows as the John Noble expresses, after the General Manager who had succeeded Allport in February of that year. The Great Northern showed how seriously it regarded this threat by putting on, within a fortnight of the opening of the Midland line, two expresses each way making the journey between Leeds and London in $3\frac{3}{4}$ hours – the best Midland trains taking $4\frac{1}{2}$.[7] To Manchester it was a similar story. The London & North Western had the shortest and incomparably the easiest route; but its management disliked high speeds and was content to provide trains that jogged along at about 45 mph. The Midland, with its climb of nearly 900 feet from Derby to Peak Forest, did the journey in the same time. And then in 1883 the Great Northern and Manchester Sheffield & Lincolnshire companies, over a route harder still and even longer, began to put on trains that were as quick. By 1888 there were three expresses leaving London for Manchester by all these routes at the same time, 2 p.m., the North Western and Great Northern trains due to arrive simultaneously at 6.15, the Midland five minutes later.[8]

The long-distance service out of St Pancras, then, showed energy and enterprise in its planning. Not quite the same could be said of the Midland suburban service. This too was competitive. Luton, Harpenden, St Albans and Mill Hill were all served by the Great Northern, St Albans by the London & North Western also; closer in, the Midland's West End (now West Hampstead) and Finchley Road stations were each within 250 yards of established stations on the Hampstead Junction line running from Willesden to Camden Road and so, by the North London, into Broad Street. Presently, moreover, the Metropolitan Company became another competitor here, when the line from Baker Street to Swiss Cottage was extended to West End Lane, a third station in West Hampstead, in 1879.

The more important suburban traffic ran from these stations not into St Pancras but on to the Metropolitan line, either to Farringdon Street and Moorgate or southwards to Ludgate Hill and the London Chatham & Dover Railway, under the terms of an agreement concluded in 1869. In

1870 St Pancras received no more than a dozen suburban trains, from Hendon, Crouch Hill, and stations to the south, each weekday; more than four times that number ran down on to the Metropolitan line. Allport anticipated 'a large suburban traffic to the districts of St Albans and Luton'.[9] Yet his company made no striking effort to stimulate it from St Pancras.

One group of services was operated out of St Pancras that has now totally disappeared: those over the Dudding Hill loop line from Brent to Acton Wells Junction and so to the District and London & South Western systems. These services were most numerous in the 'seventies, when the Midland Company clearly hoped a good deal from them, and they took forms surprising to us today. From 1878 to 1880, for example, there was a service by this line – comprising at one time seven trains a day – from St Pancras to Earl's Court. Midland trains ran to Richmond. It is curious to find a well-informed guide-book of 1879 telling the visitor to London who wants to make a pleasant excursion there, or to Acton of Kew, to go by the Midland Railway.[10] In later years these services proved totally unremunerative, and the last of them ceased in 1902, when the stations on the Dudding Hill loop were closed to passengers.[11] The line continued, however, to carry a substantial freight traffic, and it is still in use for that purpose today.

Another line, running in a north-easterly direction, proved more valuable for passenger traffic. The Tottenham & Hampstead Junction Railway – a struggling little concern authorized in 1862 – had passed under the dual control of the Midland and Great Eastern Companies in 1864; and the Midland secured powers in that year to build a short line to join it at Kentish Town. This linked the Midland and the Great Eastern at Tottenham North Junction. When it was opened in 1870 it conferred a double benefit. By means of it the Midland secured access through Stratford to the London docks, whilst the Great Eastern was able to run trains from its Cambridge main line into St Pancras – a 'West End terminus' greatly preferable to Shoreditch, or even to the much better Liverpool Street when that station was opened in 1875.

The Great Eastern worked its own service into and out of St Pancras from August 1, 1870. This included trains in each direction between St Pancras and Cambridge. In 1876 an express was put on, leaving St Pancras at 12.3 p.m. and running non-stop to Cambridge in 82 minutes. By 1904 this time was 11 minutes shorter.[12] These trains ran until the First World War. There was a quaint snobbery in Cambridge in this matter. In the Darwin circle in the 1890s a lady going up to London for the day took the 8.30 train by the Great Northern to King's Cross. 'No-one ever went to St Pancras by the Great Eastern Railway if they could help it; and Liverpool Street was unknown to the genteel'.[13] The Great Eastern Company maintained its own booking-office at St Pancras for some time. It stood facing the head of No. 2 platform.

The value of the Tottenham & Hampstead line increased in 1894, when an extension was opened from South Tottenham to Woodgrange Park on the London Tilbury & Southend Railway. This afforded the Midland Company access to southern Essex, and especially to Tilbury docks, which had been inaugurated in 1886. Equally, it gave the Tilbury Company, like the Great Eastern, a 'West End terminus' in London, valuable as an alternative to Fenchurch Street, with its many inconveniences. As soon as the line was opened, the Midland began to run a service to Southend. In 1899 the working was taken over by the Tilbury Company, whose locomotives then entered St Pancras side by side with those of the Midland and the Great Eastern. At the same time boat trains began to use St Pancras in connection with the Australian liners coming into Tilbury: a development of which there will be more to say later.

The Midland purchased the Tilbury Company outright in 1912. At the same time the Great Eastern was given powers to build a junction with its Colchester main line at Forest Gate, in order to run trains from that line into St Pancras – an indication that at that time the Cambridge-St Pancras service was profitable. But the junction was not in fact built.

*   *   *   *

For all these services, and for the beer traffic that flowed smoothly and profitably in from Burton (three complete trains a day, and more at the October brewing season),[14] the station proved ample (*ills 35-36*). The extra double-sided platform provided for in Barlow's original plan was added shortly after 1890.[15] This increased the number of platform faces to seven, as it has remained since. The new platform faces were numbered 3 and 4. Their construction was in timber, lighter than that of the original five, and these two platforms are still known traditionally as 'the wood'. In the long run, as we shall see, the platforms proved too short. That deficiency did not appear in the nineteenth century. Another, however, did.

No-one could have quarrelled with Barlow's decision to make the railway cross the Regent's Canal by an over-bridge, and therefore to build the station above the level of the Euston Road. But it was a necessary drawback to that decision that the approach to the station for road traffic had to be steep. The best way to ease the slope was to ensure that the ultimate level to be attained, that of the platforms, was as low as possible. It must have been largely for this reason that the railway was laid out on a gradient that falls into the station from Regent's Canal bridge, first at 1 in 217, and then at 1 in 440 right along the platforms to the very buffer-stops. Through this device the buffer-stops are 3 feet 3 inches lower than they would have been if the line had been brought in on a level from the bridge: an important gain for a horse dragging a cab, filled with passengers and ample Victorian luggage, up from the Euston Road. The railway gradient was not, indeed, very steep; but it was steep enough to cause difficulties with the braking of trains entering the station. Four accidents occurred, none of them fatal yet all serious enough to require investigation by Inspecting Officers of the Board of Trade, between 1891 and 1906.[16]

On each occasion the story was the same: of a train arriving in the station whose driver was unable to stop it completely, so that it ran into vehicles standing at the head of the platform or into the buffer-stops. One of these accidents, on August 12, 1894, was little more serious than the rest. It occurred to the night train from Edinburgh, running into Platform 7, thirty-five minutes late, at 8.30 a.m.[17] The rails were slippery from the droppings of a fish train, and this, so the driver claimed, prevented the brakes from working.

There was something in his contention; but the truth of the matter lay elsewhere, and the Inspecting Officers who investigated all these accidents were agreed about it. In every instance the driver had neglected the Company's rule that terminal stations should be entered at a speed low enough to enable the train to be stopped by the use of the hand-brake alone. But in three of these four cases the witnesses – signalmen and guards as well as engine-crews – were united in saying that the train entered the station as a speed no greater than usual. In other words, the rule was ignored. 'It is a notorious fact, which no person habitually using the station can fail to observe', wrote the Inspecting Officer, Major Marindin, in 1894, 'that the "*usual*" speed for trains running into St Pancras station is not five miles an hour but fifteen miles an hour and more, while not one of the officers of the Company present at my enquiry could state that, since the introduction of continuous brakes, he ever saw a train running in at so low a speed as five miles an hour, which is about what would be called hand-brake speed.'[18] On all these occasions the whole train was fitted with the automatic vacuum brake, which was unquestionably in good order. In the first and last the drivers testified that the pressure of steam in their engines had been inadequate to maintain the brake. In the last of them, and in that alone, the speed was exceptionally high, and the Inspecting Office, Major J W Pringle, came to the conclusion that the driver had applied his brakes too late: a particularly flagrant dereliction of duty since the Locomotive Superintendent, R M Deeley, had issued strict new instructions in May of the previous year, which the driver admitted he knew, requiring that in approaching a terminal station the engine must never run at more that six miles an hour when passing the head of the platform.[19] All these accidents would have caused less damage, however – one or two of them might not have occurred at all – if the station had not had to be entered on a sharply falling gradient.

Minor accidents of the same kind have continued to occur down to our own time. The last was on October 15, 1967.[20]

There was inconvenience also in the other direction. Since the line rose steadily for the first 1,000 yards out of the station, a locomotive with a heavy train found difficulty in getting away to a quick start. It was the custom for the shunting engine that had brought the empty coaches into the station to provide banking assistance in the rear; and when this was being done to some purpose the whole station re-echoed with the noise. The shunting engine then dropped off at the end of the platform, leaving the train engine – or engines, for the Midland Company frequently employed two – to battle on alone.

*   *   *   *

In the 'seventies, when St Pancras station was new, the Midland Company was widely popular with railway travellers in general, for reasons we have seen. Until the mid-eighties its services showed almost continuous improvement. 'This line is … to be admired', wrote Edward Foxwell in 1883, 'for the *uniform* excellence and symmetrical running of its trains, the roominess of its carriages, and the energy with which it has developed "through" services.'[21] By way of example he observed that 'the 5.15 a.m. newspaper train runs easily in the hour from St Pancras to Bedford, 49¾ miles, and then does the 49½ miles to Leicester in the next hour. These are the sort of things that do not happen out of England'.[22] Reviewing the progress made in the provision of express trains in Britain between 1871 and 1883, Lieut. H B Willock pointed out that it had done better in these years than any other railway save the Great Eastern. 'On this line,' he wrote, 'there has been very great progress. The number of expresses has been more than doubled, the average journey-speed is 4 miles per hour greater, and the mileage has increased 147 per cent.'[23]

Shortly after these commendations were published, however, the Midland's reputation began to grow slightly tarnished. By the turn of the century it had lost very nearly all its glamour. The main explanation of this is that the Company was offering a service on paper that it could not provide in practice.

No other London terminus has so long a history of unpunctuality in its trains as St Pancras. Every railway that operates a dense traffic to an intricate schedule is subject to disorder of this kind, and the fault may not always lie with the management. It may be due to delays a hundred miles

104

off; to necessary engineering work on the line; to the folly or eccentricity of passengers; to accident, to pure bad luck. A modicum of these things must be accepted by every railway administration, which must apologize to its customers and take the blame on its own broad shoulders.

All these things serve not only as reasons but as excuses for unpunctuality. When a railway runs into constant troubles of the kind, however, it must expect complaint to grow louder. If they are protracted over a very long period, it will make itself notorious. This is what happened in the eighties and 'nineties to the companies operating in the south-eastern corner of England. Year after year *The Times* carried crops of letters complaining of their disgraceful unpunctuality, correspondents vying with one another to see who could produce the most preposterous example. Foxwell called this unpunctuality a 'monstrosity', adding truly that 'trains which never (well, hardly ever) throughout the year arrive decently near their time are maddening to every one except the officials; there is no point in them, they have lost their savour and are as different from the real article as a stale egg from a fresh one'.[24]

The misdoings of the Midland were never of that order; but they were frequent enough to provoke repeated criticism. As early as 1870 the Board thought it right to appoint a commttee to inquire into the reasons for the want of punctuality in the Company's trains.[25] The decision to admit third-class passengers to all Midland trains in 1872 was thought by some people to have made punctual running harder to achieve because the passengers could not be got into and out of crowded carriages on time.[26] Foxwell himself spoke, in the 'eighties, of the 'gross and notorious unpunctuality of some of the most important Midland expresses (e.g. the Scotch)'.[27] That phrase has been echoed again and again in the years that have gone by since. Acworth discussed the shortcomings of the up night trains from Scotland.[28] When recorders of railway speed began to multiply in the nineties their runs on the Midland line usually began with a late start or included serious delays *en route*.[29] The Company was so gravely perturbed by this irregularity that it appointed a major Commission of Inquiry into Train Delays in 1891. This was at work for two years – and very hard, producing no less that eighty-two reports in all.[30] Each of these usually dealt with the causes of delay at a particular point. St Pancras was never the subject of a specific inquiry, but some notion of the scale of the disorder is given by the evidence in its 42nd report that in the early months of 1892 the average delay to trains on the last $11\frac{1}{2}$ miles into London was 521 hours a week.

With a view to bringing the timetables into a nearer accordance with reality, the Company slowed down some of its bookings – to the scorn of Acworth, who complained that it had 'taught us the use of the word "decelerate"'.[31] Then, in 1901, it made an effort to regain some of the Edinburgh traffic it had lost to its competitors, and provoked what might have been a third Race to Scotland, like those of 1888 and 1895. It was a ludicrous failure. That was due not to its partner the North British, which performed admirably beyond Carlisle, but to the Midland's own unpunctuality, which grew worse as the 'race' progressed, until it was obliged to abandon the challenge with ignominy.[32] Next year the Company set out to secure a larger share of the London-Manchester traffic. The effort was greeted by the *Railway Engineer* with hoots of laughter:

> 'The fast express trains which the Midland Railway Company have put on to "compete" with the London & North Western service to Manchester may be strongly recommended to those who have the misfortune to possess a sluggish liver, and want it agitated. They are light trains and expresses only on paper. Mr Rous-Marten "observed" one which was stopped or checked by signal ten times on the down journey, and six times besides at every box from Kentish Town to St Pancras on the up journey. As this is the usual way of conducting this "competition", no-one will be surprised to hear that Sir Ernest Paget [the Midland Chairman] is anxious to come to some arrangement with the North Western.'[33]

37. The station in the early 1960s, before the concourse was enlarged. The seven platform layout dated from the early 1890s. The upper plan shows the undercroft.

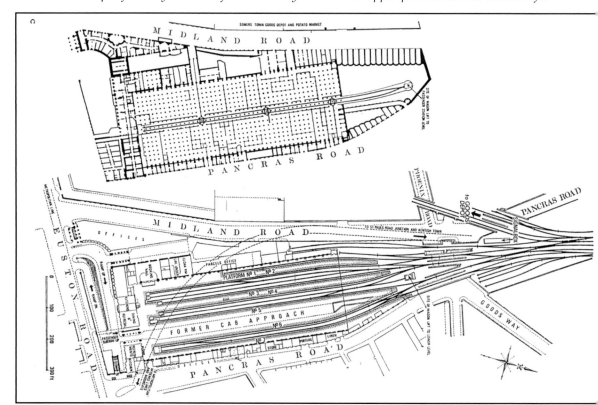

In the following year, 1902, the Midland Company announced that it was going to instal water-troughs at Oakley, Manton, and Loughborough. Again it was derided in the same quarter. 'The immediate object of these troughs', wrote the *Railway Engineer*, 'is to run trains to Manchester and Leeds without stopping – at least, to indicate in the timetables the possibility of such events taking place – because we have never had the good fortune to travel by a Midland express that did not stop many more times that it was supposed to do.'[34]

Such examples could be multiplied down the years. For whereas the much worse crimes of the south-eastern companies were eventually expunged when their lines were electrified, from 1909 onwards, the Midland line to St Pancras has borne a bad reputation, intermittently if not continuously, down to our own time. The running on it was atrociously irregular in the latter days of steam traction.[35] British Railways could defend themselves by saying that the motive power available was unsatisfactory: the locomotives themselves were more than adequate for their work, but they were wretchedly maintained. Why then did they repeat the ancient mistake of the Midland by introducing a new smart timetable in 1957, to schedules that they were unable to keep? In the late 1960s travellers on the line usually had little cause to complain on that score, except those who used the 'Thames-Clyde Express' to and from Glasgow, the successor of the Midland's daytime Scotchman. Its 'gross and notorious unpunctuality', on a schedule of interminable slowness, with locomotives more powerful than any ever used on the line before, continued: so much so that in 1967 the up train had to be given longer still to perform the journey.[36]

Over the years, then, many thousands of passengers have looked up, on their arrival, at the huge clock at St Pancras and noted with annoyance how late they were; many thousands of their friends, coming to meet them, have learnt the full meaning of the term 'waiting rooms'. Why should this be? Besides the general causes of unpunctuality in trains, which have already been mentioned, what has made this line so especially unreliable? Is the cause to be attributed in any sense at all to St Pancras station itself?

Before 1948 one cause could be said to be the tradition set up by the Midland Company, from the very thinking that had led to the construction of its line to London: the desire to compete with established rivals, but on disadvantageous terms. Its route was immeasurably harder to work, abounding in stiff gradients and sharp curves, and to all large towns north and west of Sheffield it was longer. No less important, a Midland express served not merely one or two large towns in the distance, but a number of others on the way. Between King's Cross and Leeds the line runs through no place larger than Doncaster; on the Midland line lie Leicester, Nottingham, and Sheffield. Only a very few expresses could afford to pass one of them by without stopping. Yet the Midland persisted in trying to ignore these drawbacks. If the effort has a touch of the heroic about it, which one is constrained to admire, it must be recognized that, in rational terms, it represented a striving after something scarcely attainable.

Moreover, throughout its history the passenger traffic carried by the line has been less important than that in goods and minerals – above all, until very recent years, the traffic in coal. The line was at all times heavily occupied, and a relatively high proportion of the trains moved slowly. The obvious remedy was to increase the number of tracks, and this was adopted, until there were four tracks for the whole 75 miles from St Pancras to Glendon South Junction, where the new Nottingham line of 1880 diverged from the old main line. The importance of the freight traffic was emphasized by an arrangement almost peculiar to the Midland Company. North of Bedford the new tracks, on the east side, were reserved for goods trains; no passenger platforms were built on them save at Wellingborough and Kettering. It is open to question whether or not this was a satisfactory plan. It certainly worked to the disadvantage of the passenger trains by confining them rigidly, fast and slow alike, to a single pair of rails.

Other causes too may be adduced to show why the Midland trains always had difficulty in running to time – Acworth instances the multiplicity of connections to be maintained and the special problems presented by the fish traffic.[37] All these difficulties occurred far outside St Pancras station. There was, however, one that arose from the station itself.

In planning it, Barlow and his colleagues had looked a long way ahead. The single-span roof had given the Company the utmost possible flexibility in the use it made of the space inside. The original five platforms having been increased to seven, it would have been difficult – though not quite impossible – to add more within the shed; and to extend it laterally with a supplementary station (as at Manchester Central) would have been awkward and very costly. In the long run, however, this did not prove very important. The station was deficient not so much in breadth as in length.

When it was built, trains were very short, and at a time of pressure two, or even three, could stand at each of the main platforms – following the practice already established in the Brighton station at Victoria. Nothing strikes one more forcibly in the early prints of St Pancras than the diminutive size of the trains, crawling in and out of their vast hall. But in the succeeding years the trains grew substantially larger. True, the Midland's decision to abolish second class meant, of itself, some reduction, since only two classes of carriages had to be provided, instead of three. But that gain had been offset in the previous year by the introduction of Pullman cars, which the Company included in most of its best expresses to the North.

Though they did not establish themselves permanently on the Midland – Pullman's contract with the Company expired in 1888 and was not renewed[38] - sleeping and dining cars, on the normal British pattern, evolved out of them. The corridor established itself on ordinary trains in the 'nineties. It occupied space previously available for seating, which meant that, in order to carry the same number of passengers, more vehicles had to be employed.[39]

For all these reasons, and because the number of passenger journeys was increasing steadily with the increase of the population itself, the average train became heavier and longer. The provision of passenger space grew more and more generous. Early in the twentieth century the Midland was building sleeping cars that weighed 37 tons apiece and carried only 11 passengers. Each of these cars was 65 feet long.[40] Put three of them into a train with the ordinary coaches and mail vans that would usually be marshalled with them, add an engine at each end, and one of the St Pancras platforms was nearly filled.

This difficulty did not become pressing very quickly. It was the Midland Company's policy to run frequent light express trains rather than a smaller number of heavy ones – the practice followed by its neighbour the Great Northern; and the suburban traffic into and out of St Pancras had remained on a modest scale. But it was still true, nevertheless, that only three, or at the most four, incoming trains could be accommodated in the station at one time; and if – in the summer season, for example – extra trains were run, or if through delays on the line there were trains wishing to enter the station out of course, they might well be held up outside for want of platform space.

In the years between the two Wars trains grew again in size, and it then became a serious nuisance that no train of more than twelve coaches could stand at any of the St Pancras platforms. A thirteen-coach train, with its engine, stood over the points and blocked movement into and out of the station on its east or west side. And by this time expresses of fifteen, sixteen, or even more coaches were a daily sight on other lines. As at two others of the stations built at the same time, Charing Cross and Cannon Street, though for different reasons, there was a bottleneck at the end of the platforms, which made it impossible to lengthen them. It was now that the unhappy proximity of the gasworks and old St Pancras churchyard became so important, limiting the number of tracks that could be provided in the space between them and confining the station itself to the south.

At times of heavy traffic this limitation remains serious, though for a number of reasons – including a reduction in the seating-space available to many second-class passengers in recent years – it is only occasionally troublesome today. It would not be fair to argue that Barlow and his colleagues were short-sighted in failing to estimate the growth in the size of trains during the succeeding century, for this arose largely from factors that were not foreseeable in their time.

All in all, the station proved itself, in everyday use, a satisfactory instrument for the purposes it was designed to serve. Alone among the principal Victorian stations of London, St Pancras has never been altered in any matter of importance since it was built *(ill. 37)*.

*   *   *   *

This is, in truth, a great tribute to the station's design: for the volume of traffic grew steadily and almost without interruption throughout the life of the Company that built it. We can trace that growth year by year from 1872 to 1922.[42] In 1872 there were 171,000 passenger bookings at the station, and the total 'coaching receipts' (including horses, carriages, dogs and the conveyance of parcels) amounted to £97,000. With a few fluctuations in the 'eighties, both rose steadily until 1907, when they had increased approximately fivefold.[43] The upward trend was resumed in 1913 and continued, with a setback in the exceptional war years 1917-18, until bookings passed the million mark in 1919. The peak year was 1920, with 1,189,000 bookings and coaching receipts of £887,000; but the figures for the last year, 1922, were only a little lower.

The same documents give us the total working expenses of the station, and they run to a different pattern. They started off at £9,600 and rose slowly – at a lower rate than the receipts – to £36,000 in 1901. A reorganization then removed the parcels traffic to another jurisdiction, and the working expenses fell in 1902 by nearly 30 per cent. They stayed at that level or lower for fifteen years, rising at a startling rate from 1918 onwards.

These working expenses consisted chiefly of salaries and wages. One would like to know more than one can about the men and women who worked the station and the hotel. A mass of detailed information concerning the railway staff is given in two volumes of the Midland Company's records, covering the years 1876–1908, listing each employee, from the Stationmaster downwards, by name, with his pay and the date of any change made in it.[44] They do not, however, enable one to reckon at all accurately what the normal establishment was, or how it grew with the growing volume of traffic.

The records need some care in handling. It is possible to say that throughout this long period the porters at St Pancras were paid between 16s and 21s a week, with a normal wage of 19s in the early twentieth century. (But what did they earn in tips? That is something no-one will ever know.) There was not, however, a standard wage, nor were there, in general, any regular increments. There might even be reductions. In January 1879 the Midland Company lowered the wages of certain classes of its servants – including passenger guards – earning 17s a week and more. This provoked a strike, in passenger guards – in which the men were defeated.[45] Advancement depended largely on length of service, so that the range of salaries earned within a particular grade might be considerable. Booking clerks got anything between £60 and £140 a year. Some quite responsible men were paid surprisingly low wages: ticket examiners, for instance, received only 23s-28s a week, guards only 32s-45s. Nor were the top salaries impressive. The Chief Booking Clerk was earning £175 in 1876, £300 thirty years later. The Stationmaster himself received only £265 in 1876, rising to £500 in 1897 and remaining at that figure for at least ten years.

Unfortunately this detailed record comes to an end in 1907. We have no such information for the last fifteen years of the Midland Company's life, and no records in any way comparable have been preserved from the subsequent rule of the London Midland & Scottish Railway. There was strikingly little upward movement in the working expenses of the station until 1917. In 1916, indeed, they were exactly £3,000 less than they had been nine years earlier: the station was less well staffed in war-time, and some of the men had been replaced by women, whose wages were lower. But in 1917 working expenses began to rise steeply. By August 1920 the average wages of all grades of railway workers were estimated to have risen by about 180 per cent compared with the rates paid at the outbreak of war in 1914.[46]

* * * *

Our information about the staff running the station is, then, imperfect. About the staff of the hotel we also know very little. However, the census returns for 1881 and 1891 reveal that it was generously staffed, as was only to be expected for a building dependent on coal fires and ill-equipped with bathrooms and lavatories. In 1881, there were 115 staff recorded, a high proportion of them Swiss or German. Ten years later, there were 145, more of whom were British born. In both censuses, which were taken on Sunday nights, hotel servants exceeded the number of guests. The utmost secrecy was observed from the very outset about the hotel branch of the Company's business. As we have seen, there had been long controversy about the completion of the building and about the wisdom of keeping its management in the Company's hands. The Directors and the most prominent shareholders were divided about these matters: Edward Baines, for example declared in 1869 that he had always been opposed to the building of the hotel from the beginning.[47] (But it must be recognized that he had an axe of his own to grind: he was among the most conspicuous teetotallers of his time.) Shortly afterwards E S Ellis was writing privately to the Company's Accountant to ask for particulars of the earnings of the Company's other hotels, as well as of the receipts of Messrs Spiers & Pond, the caterers who rented many of the Midland refreshment rooms, including those at St Pancras.[48]

When the hotel was opened, partially in 1873 and completely three years later, it fell to Ellis as Chairman to deal with the inevitable questions about its revenue and expenditure that shareholders put at the Company's half-yearly meetings. He consistently refused to give them any precise information. He was a most straightforward man, neither evasive nor prone to secrecy. His Board had clearly decided that, in the hotly competitive business of hotel management, as little as possible ought to be given away. Some of the other hotels at the London terminal stations were owned by separate companies, and these were obliged to publish at least some information about the state of their business, if only by the dividends they declared. When the shareholders were debating the Directors' recommendation to go ahead with the first stage of the hotel in 1869, the Chairman, Hutchinson, was able to point, in support of this policy, to the 8 per cent that the Grosvenor Hotel was paying, the 10 per cent of the Charing Cross.[49] No such in formation was ever supplied in respect of the Midland Grand, whose printed accounts were inextricably involved with those of the other hotels owned and run by the Company; nor do the surviving unpublished records enable us to isolate it from its fellows.

Ellis was first asked the question when only Stage I of the hotel had been built. He replied that 'the income considerably exceeds the expenditure' and that he hoped that, when the whole was completed, it would offer a very fair return on the Company's outlay.[50] Six months later he felt able to be a little more enthusiastic. It was answering the expectations of the Directors, he said, and 'during several months lately it has been filled to overflowing'.[51] In 1878, the entire hotel being in working order, though he again refused to disclose any exact figures he stated that earnings had increased and that it would yield a satisfactory return, 'besides accommodating and bringing to your system a large amount of traffic'.[52] During the rest of that year the prosperity of the hotel increased, so as to afford the Company 'a very handsome net revenue'. But Ellis felt it necessary to warn the shareholders that business was falling off in the opening months of 1879, as it had in other London hotels. This he attributed to the weather[53] – they were going through a particularly severe winter; but the underlying cause was the disastrous slump, hitting first agriculture, then industry and the general trade of the country, in the late 1870s.

Ellis's practice of withholding all precise information about the Company's hotel business was continued by his successors. When a shareholder tried to extract some figures out of M W Thompson, for example, in 1889, he was told that the Midland hotels paid, but the Chairman was not prepared to disclose any details of their working and management.[54]

The Company took great pains to ensure, as far as possible, the comfort of its guests. The southern screen that Scott had insisted upon to insulate the hotel from the station's noise and smoke proved effective. Much trouble was caused, however, by noise from the roads outside. Complaints became serious in 1875 respecting the traffic passing under the eastern archway from the main arrival platforms. Etzenberger was then instructed to consult india-rubber manufacturers, to see if they could propose a remedy.[55] Messrs Mackintosh came up with samples of rubber flooring, and a portion of this was laid under the arch, by way of experiment.[56] It does not seem to have been entirely successful. Was it perhaps slippery in wet weather? When the western wing was completed and the guests had to be protected from the same nuisance arising from the road underneath, it was decided to re-pave it with wooden block, Messrs. Mackintosh supplying india-rubber strips to be placed between them. This arrangement was adopted also for the new main entrance to the hotel, at the south-western corner of the building. The total cost of it was a little over £900.[57]

These measures may have gone as far as possible towards solving the problem. Another arose, however, when the new part of the hotel was brought into use: for some of the guests' rooms now abutted closely on to the Euston Road. This was paved, like most London streets at the time, with granite setts, which echoed with a ringing clarity the noise of the horses' hooves. The remedy for this disturbance lay with the St Pancras Vestry, which was responsible for the maintenance of the road; but nothing was done until, in 1880, the Midland Company offered a contribution of £1,000 towards the cost of replacing the setts, in the stretch of road opposite the hotel, by wooden blocks, which had evidently answered satisfactorily on its own premises. The offer was accepted, and the work carried through in 1881.[58]

The Company was proud of its hotel, and looked after its interests with care: perhaps we should say rather that it gave its managers all the support they needed. Etzensberger left in 1884 and was succeeded by William Towle, who had been in the Company's service for twenty years and was Manager of the Midland Hotel at Derby. He gradually added to his responsibilities the control of the other big provincial hotels acquired or built by the Company at Liverpool, Leeds, Bradford, Heysham, and Manchester. He and his family managed the Hotels Department down to the end of the

38. *The hotel coffee room after the alterations of 1904. Compare with illustration 27.*

Midland Company's days and continued under its successor the London Midland & Scottish.[59]

The Midland Grand always bore a good reputation throughout its life. At first it was expensive. For a room, breakfast, dinner, and attendance it charged 14s a night in 1879.[60] This made it the dearest of all the railway hotels save the Great Northern, whose charges were the same, and only 6d less than the opulent Langham in Portland Place. Its *table d'hôte* dinner, at 5s, was selected for special mention at the same time (alone among those provided by railway hotels); and – in a select company, which again included the Langham – it was recommended for 'large dinners, where expense is no object and a good private room is a desideratum'.[61]

The London hotel business expanded rapidly in the 'eighties, and the Midland Grand sank back from a position of pre-eminence into one of solid, consistently good reputation. It always stayed in the front rank of those maintained by railway companies. Efforts were made to upgrade its facilities, for instance by installing electricity in 1885-7 and the addition of more bathrooms in 1905-12. A new dining room called the Venetian Room was inserted at the end of the Midland Road wing for the use of tour parties and special dinners. Gradually, as redecoration took place, the high Victorian flamboyance of the main public rooms and bedrooms was toned down, in an attempt to keep abreast of changing tastes. The main staircase was re-decorated in 1901, and T. Wallis Hay's fresco *The Garden of Deduit* added: three years later the Coffee Room was given a new treatment, including the whitening of the cornice and beams *(ill. 38)*.[62] In 1911 Baedeker described it as 'one of the best of the large terminal hotels', with 400 beds and charges a trifle lower than they had been when it was swaggeringly new: the price of dinner remained at 5s, but full *pension* could now be had for 12s a night.[63] In the first edition of the *Blue Guide to London*, published at the end of the First World War, the Midland Grand shared with the Great Eastern, and with no other railway-owned hotel, the distinction of a star.[64] As late as 1930 it was still starred by Baedeker – again with the Great Eastern. Its charges were then 8s 6d and upwards for a room (with private bath, 15s), 4s for breakfast, 5s for lunch, and 7s 6d for dinner.[65]

By that time, however, the hotel was nearing its end. In the early twentieth century it remained profitable, but much less so than the Midland Railway's hotels in Manchester, Liverpool and Leeds. The solidity of its construction, the very grandeur of its design, made it hard to adapt it to the changing demands of the new century. The lack of a sufficient number of private bathrooms, and the difficulty of adding more, was one of the reasons why the London Midland & Scottish Company decided to close it down in 1935. It was then converted into offices, and in that form it continued until the

1980s *(ill. 40)*. During its working life as a hotel, the Midland Grand seldom featured in the social pages of the press as its West End rivals did: however solid its reputation, it was not a great venue for celebratory banquets or parties. On a more sombre note, it was at the hotel that Sir James Allport died in 1892, loyal to his creation at the last; and in five years it witnessed the death of George Gilbert Scott Junior, the talented but pathetic son of the architect who had designed it.[66]

* * * *

For St Pancras station, as for so much else in England, the First World War was the herald of change. Perhaps it would not be fanciful to say that that change was signalled on the night of February 17, 1918, when five bombs were dropped by German aeroplanes on or near the station and hotel. One of these fell in Midland Road, close to the south-eastern corner of Somers Town goods station. Two fell on the terrace in front of the hotel, another on the western tower. None of these four caused any casualties. But the fifth, which landed on the glass-roofed carriage approach beside the booking-office, killed twenty people and injured thirty-three. This was the greatest number of casualties suffered in any air-raid on a London station during that war. The raid caused no interruption at all, however, to the running of the trains inside.[67] One consequence of the raid was the loss of

39. Waiting near Platform 5 in the 1920s

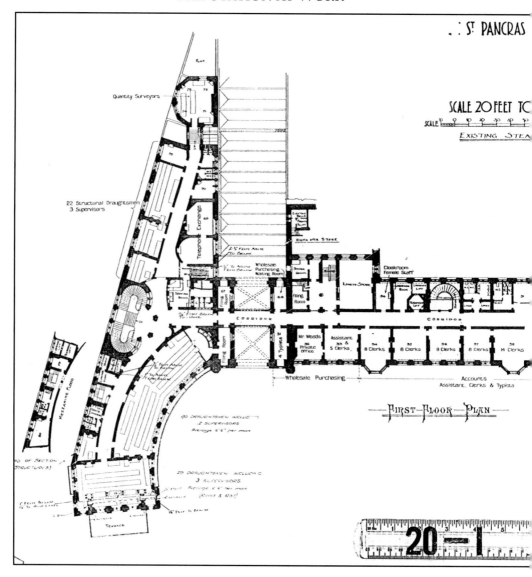

40. *Plan of the hotel in office use, 1945*

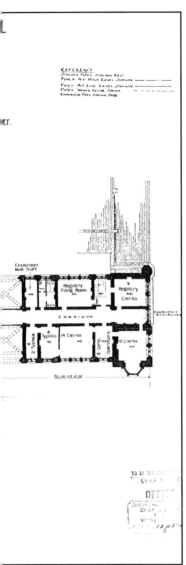

Scott's Booking Hall roof, which was replaced by a much plainer ceiling supported from timber Belfast trusses.

The war ended with the railway system deplorably run down, after four years of increasing strain; and much was heard of plans for re-casting their management. This discussion centred chiefly on their ownership and administration – ought they to continue under the government control imposed during the war, nationalized for good, or should they be returned to private enterprise? A part of it was concerned, however, with matters of planning, in the period of reconstruction that lay ahead; and this threw up a number of proposals for drastic change in traffic routes. It was now that it was suggested, for the first time, that St Pancras station should be closed and its traffic diverted elsewhere.

This proposal was made by the London Society, in a report edited by Sir Aston Webb (a figure from another world indeed!) and published in 1921. Nine of the main London stations should be closed, it argued. The traffic handled at King's Cross and St Pancras could be diverted to Euston – apparently by making fresh use of the North London line. St Pancras would then 'cease to be more than an hotel'.[68]

This remained a pipe-dream, and nothing more. When the dust of the post-war controversies had settled, the only substantial changes that had emerged from them were in management, with the setting-up of the four large mainline companies through the Railways Act of 1921. Under its terms the Midland Railway, and with it St Pancras station, passed under the control of the London Midland & Scottish Company at midnight on December 31, 1922.

The change made little immediate difference. At first indeed, on the face of it, the

Midland appeared to have absorbed its companions, even the mighty London & North Western. In the new company, in many things, Midland practices prevailed; and that seemed to be symbolized by the adoption of its rich crimson livery for the passenger locomotives and rolling-stock of the new combine. But the Midland had been nourished on competition, and had thrived on it. The Railways Act weakened the force of competition. Under its operation the services in which the Midland had competed with the London & North Western (now its partner) were reduced or eliminated; and, of the two, it was generally the North Western services that were favoured. By 1939 there were only two down trains, and one up, with through coaches between St Pancras and Liverpool – a sensible change, since the route was 25 miles longer than the North Western, but one that hit Leicester, Nottingham, and Derby. Through carriages still ran from St Pancras to Heysham, in connection with the night boat for Belfast; but few people can have travelled all the way in them, since the Ulster Express left from Euston, to connect with the same boat, two hours later in the evening. As for the Scottish services, by 1939 they had been pared down to two day and two night trains, serving Glasgow and Edinburgh, and nowhere beyond. The Midland had provided, by arrangement with the Scottish companies, through carriages to Stranraer, to Greenock, to Aberdeen and Inverness. All these now disappeared. The last to go were those to Aberdeen, in 1932.[69]

Of the old competitive spirit, something, however remained. As late as 1939, in quite the old style, two trains still left St Pancras and Marylebone simultaneously at 4.55 p.m., to reach Bradford at 8 o'clock and 8.1 respectively. St Pancras offered the best service to Sheffield and a service to Leeds which, if a little slower than that from King's Cross, was in some other respects more convenient.[70] The services to the great East Midland towns provided from St Pancras were adequate, although unenterprising, down to 1937. Then they were suddenly transformed, to reach a point of excellence quite unattainable by those from Marylebone. To Leicester, for example, there were fourteen expresses taking an average time of 108 minutes for the 99-mile journey – four of them making it in exactly 99 minutes.[71]

The Cambridge services were never put back after the First World War; and only a very few trains ran from St Pancras to Southend. The boat trains still ran, however, to and from Tilbury, with one interesting, though short-lived, addition. Before the war, in 1913, there had been a plan to operate a night service to and from Ostend via Tilbury, the Belgian government being incensed at the heavy taxes imposed by the Dover Harbour Board to pay for the new Marine station there. This came to nothing; but it was revived in another form in 1930 when a French company, the Alsace-Lorraine-

Angleterre, began to operate a service between Tilbury and Dunkirk. One argument in favour of this enterprise had been the convenience with which passengers from the North of England could reach the Continent. By travelling up to St Pancras and walking a few yards there they could step into the boat train, without the tiresome necessity of crossing London to Victoria. But the service was not a success. Having run for two years only, it was transferred to Folkestone. There too it failed to establish itself, and in 1936 it gave place to the train-ferry, operated from a specially-constructed dock at Dover. The ancestry of the Night Ferry can thus be traced back to St Pancras in 1930.

* * * *

The Second World War intensified the changes brought about by the first. The station was damaged in many more air-raids and its traffic much more seriously dislocated – though none of them caused so many deaths as that of February 1918. The first three occurred within the space of a month in the autumn of 1940; as a result of one of them the station was closed entirely for five days.[72] The most serious was that in the night of May 10, 1941, when five bombs fell on the station (ill. 41). One of them, of 1,000 lb., fell at the head of Platforms 3 and 4, penetrated straight through the vault below and exploded close to the side wall of the tunnel carrying the line down to the Metropolitan, in the solid London clay. As in the bombing raid of 1918, the Booking Hall roof was badly damaged. The station was completely closed for a week; Platforms 2 and 3 were not brought back into use until June 7th.[73]

In consequence of all this damage, when the war was over the roof needed heavy repairs to restore it to its old condition. The opportunity was taken to redisbribute the glazing. To Barlow's design it had run in a single band down the centre of the train-shed, the lower parts being slated. Now it was altered to run in four narrower bands: a distinct improvement, giving a steadier natural light, better diffused throughout the interior of the building. The whole of the concourse, too, was glazed.[74] The glass in the north and south screens has never been replaced.

The station emerged from the long ordeal in 1945, like most of its fellows, in a very shabby condition, and with an uncertain future before it. While the war was still being fought, the London planners began to talk once more of its elimination. The *County of London Plan* of 1943 suggested 'that on reconstruction Euston might include the facilities of St Pancras', though without indicating, in physical terms, how this was to be accomplished.[75] For the moment, however, such large schemes lay in the distant future; and the British Transport Commission, in the years of its difficult

41. After the air-raid on 10 May 1941.

early growth, was in no condition to undertake projects of such magnitude. For a time there was even a move in the opposite direction. The *Development Plan* for the County of London of 1951 contradicted its predecessor. So far from wishing to see St Pancras station removed, it included among 'works of first priority' the electrification of the line out to St Albans or Luton.[76] A diagrammatic map was published in the *Plan* showing the volume of traffic at each of the principal London stations; and St Pancras appeared there as handling a markedly larger volume of traffic than King's Cross.

The line was not electrified; but on January 1, 1960, a new service of multiple-unit diesel trains was introduced between St Pancras and Bedford. The old suburban service had always been half-hearted – ludicrously inadequate by the standards of the electrified railways south of the Thames. Gaps of an hour and a quarter between trains were by no means uncommon, and at the still fairly rural stations beyond Luton there were several that were much longer. In 1959 a passenger for Harlington who missed the 7.20 p.m. at St Pancras, for example, was well advised to catch the 7.55 to Luton and then walk the intervening eight miles: it was quicker than waiting for the next train at 10 p.m., which (after running non-stop to St

42. A Midland Pullman.

Albans) sauntered into Harlington at 11.6. A much better service arrived now. Luton, for instance got two trains an hour from St Pancras – fifty-seven in the whole day. Better, but still well below the standards set by the Southern Region. There Guildford – the same distance from London, but a town much less than half Luton's size – had 101 trains in the day from Waterloo. Even now, St Pancras has never seen a really intensive service.

In the same year, 1960, St Pancras introduced the British traveller to a new type of train: the Pullman express with diesel engines built into it, on the model of the Italian Elettrotreni and the Trans-Europ Expresses (*ill. 42*). This 'Midland Pullman' ran up from Manchester Central at 8.50 in the morning and back from St Pancras at 6.10 at night, taking just over 3 hours 10 minutes over the journey with a single stop at Cheadle Heath. The six-coach train was for first-class passengers only, who paid a supplementary charge of £1. (What would Allport have said to that?) It was heavily patronized. Later, it began to make a mid-day trip out to Leicester, Loughborough, and Nottingham and back. This was never much used on the down service but attracted gradually-increasing custom on the up journey early in the evening.

It was the swan song of the classic Midland route to Manchester through Matlock and Peak Forest. As soon as the line from Euston had been electrified, another train took its place by that route. The Midland Pullman made its last journey on April 15, 1966. We cannot expect that St Pancras, which saw the first Pullman cars in Britain, will ever see any more.

During the lifetime of that train St Pancras became the chief point of departure from London to Manchester. The fast trains were, however, withdrawn directly the Euston electrification had been completed. All the stations between Matlock and Chinley were shut down in 1967 and notice given of the intention to close that entire stretch of line.

To enable St Pancras to handle this increased traffic, some reconstruction and improvement were undertaken. The whole track was renewed for a distance of 240 yeards out of the station in 1947.[77] Ten years later an elaborate new system of signalling was installed, with a completely new signalbox, replacing three old ones. The gantry that had long stood close to the platform ends – at one time it bore forty-two semaphore signals – now disappeared.[78] The facilities provided for passengers were also taken in hand. The refreshment service had been dislocated by the war. In 1955 it was pleasantly observed that 'the café-bar in one corner [of the concourse] looks like one part of a set from a Soho revue which has been left carelessly in the church scene from *Much Ado About Nothing*'.[79] The blowsiness of the whole south end of the station, presided over by shrieking advertisements, had been well caught at this time by the Danish artist Ebbe Sadolin.[80]

Now all this was tidied up. A new enquiry office was first provided, in 1956.[81] This led out of the booking-hall, which was itself reconstructed in the following year, with some tenderness for Scott's memory, though the timber and glass roof, damaged by bombing in 1918 and 1941, could never be replaced.[82] The roof was now a plain concrete affair, resting on a steel framework; the original booking-office, with its linenfold panelling, was retained. The jolly sculptured figures on the corbels of the north wall still looked down on a scene not too unfamiliar to them; though they must have regretted the subsequent decision to mar the walls opposite with a series of metal luggage-lockers, ugly and in the dreariest sense utilitarian.

The old buffet and restaurant arrangements were swept away in 1959, to give place to the Midland Cafeteria, the London Bar, and the Shires Restaurant.[83] The last stage of this refurbishing arrived in 1963, when the concourse – uncomfortably crowded with passengers in queues at times of heavy traffic – was a little enlarged, and the old barriers at the platform ends replaced by a new set of very decent design, firmly of their own age yet well mannered towards everything around them.[84]

That completed the work. By the late 1960s the whole station was furnished in a seemly manner, and was in fair trim. A tiny touch of bright fresh colour was introduced when the iron plates proclaiming that the Butterley Company made the ribs of the roof were painted a strong blue.

Dare we hope that when that roof next needs repainting a sky blue may once more be used – the colour eventually accepted by Barlow and Scott, under the strong, persuasive pressure of Allport?

*   *   *   *

A word or two should be said of the locomotives that have worked the traffic into and out of St Pancras over these hundred years. When the station was opened, the main-line trains were hauled chiefly by Matthew Kirtley's little single-drivers of the 25 class and by his new 2-4-0s (156 class), with 6 feet 2½ inch wheels. The singles quickly proved unequal to the work, but the coupled engines were multiplied, in various forms, culminating in the 800 and 890 classes, with driving wheels 6 inches larger *(ill. 43)*. The 890s were still being turned out after their designer's death in 1873. Kirtley's engines were extraordinarily well built, and had a very long life. His 0-4-4 tank engines, for the suburban service, were still to be seen at St Pancras in the 1930s. One of the first batch of the 156 class, turned out in 1866, was not withdrawn until 1948.

Kirtley was succeeded as the Company's Locomotive Superintendent by

43. A Kirtley 2-4-0 express engine, of the type introduced c.1870.

44. An S W Johnson 4-2-2 express engine, photographed at St Pancras, 1901.

45. A St Albans train in St Pancras station, 1959.

*46. Express trains ready to leave St Pancras 1957. The middle two are headed by
Jubilee Class 4-6-0s.*

S W Johnson: as fine a practical engineer as Kirtley, and one of the true art-
ists in locomotive design. The highest achievement of the Victorians in the
visual arts may well be thought to lie not in their painting, their furniture or
textiles, but in such engineering triumphs as the St Pancras roof and in some
of their great machines. Among these Johnson's locomotives for the Midland Railway take a very high place – perhaps the highest *(ill. 44)*.[85]

He abandoned Kirtley's double frames, and for fourteen years built nothing but coupled engines – some with a pair of leading wheels, some with
bogies – for express work. For suburban services he continued to favour
the 0-4-4 tank type. Like some other engineers he turned back to the express engine with single driving wheels in the 1880s, after a series of ex-
periments with a new steam sanding gear that applied sand to the wheels
to counteract slipping on wet or greasy rails; and in 1887 he produced the
first of the splendid 4-2-2 engines that are among the glories of the Victorian
age. Ninety-five of these machines were built in all in 1887-1900. They
were not only supremely graceful: they were efficient. It was one of these
engines that gave Charles Rous-Marten – who knew the railways of the
world as well as any man of his time – his first experience of travelling at 90
mph, in 1897.[86] One of these machines is now on exhibition at the National
Railway Museum in York.

Other companies' trains, as we have see, were by now being worked into St Pancras. The Great Eastern expresses from Cambridge were hauled by a variety of engines: Robert Sinclair's 7 foot singles, the 4-4-0s designed by Johnson before he went from the Great Eastern Company to the Midland, the 6 feet 1 inch 4-4-0s rebuilt by Adams, curiously but successfully, from Sinclair's goods engines. The through trains to the Tilbury line were worked for the first five years by Midland engines, stationed at Shoeburyness. Thereafter, from 1899 onwards, the Tilbury Company took them over, using its 4-4-2 tank engines for the purpose. When the grandiose Tilbury 4-6-4 tanks appeared in 1912, they proved too heavy for the bridges between Barking and Fenchurch Street, and they spent most of their lives working in and out of St Pancras – in the 1920s mainly on local trains to Luton.

Johnson continued to build his singles until very nearly the end of his working life; but the weight of express trains increased greatly in the 'nineties, and more powerful locomotives were called for. He met the demand with two types of 4-4-0 engine. The first, introduced in 1900, represented an enlargement of his earlier designs. With two inside cylinders, it was a strong, efficient example of the established type of British express engine. The second, which appeared a year later, was a three-cylinder compound engine. Since no entirely successful compound locomotives had yet run in this country – though the system was well established on the Continent – this was a brave experiment; and it was one that triumphantly succeeded. For the Johnson compounds, when modified by his successor R M Deeley, proved admirable machines. They at once took over the responsibility for the heaviest expresses and remained in almost sole charge of them until the 1930s. Five were built at first, then forty more, then another 195 from 1924 onwards under the London Midland & Scottish Railway, which used them all over its system, from London and Bristol to Aberdeen. When they too, in their turn, were outclassed by the more and more exacting demands made upon them, they were superseded by the 4-6-0s designed by W A (later Sir William) Stanier: the two-cylinder mixed-traffic engines and the three-cylinder 'Jubilees', which from 1937 to 1960 were the St Pancras express engines *par excellence (ill. 46)*. They were swift and powerful and wholly in command of their work until their closing years, when they were ill maintained and not always well handled by their crews. The 0-4-4 tank engines had given place to much bigger machines of the 2-6-2 and 2-6-4 types, still operating a somewhat leisurely suburban service. 4-4-2 tank engines from the Tilbury line still appeared in the 1930s. The boat trains to Tilbury Docks were almost always worked by the large six-coupled goods engines of class 4: an adequate arrangement, for those trains were always dismally slow.

In the very last years of steam operation the St Pancras expresses were handled chiefly by the big 'Royal Scots' and by the British Railways 'Britannia' Pacifics of 1951: both excellent types, amply able to fulfil all normal demands made on them as long as they were well maintained. But they were on their way out, and that condition was less and less often met. For a long time in the 1950s one of the experimental diesel locomotives ordered by the London Midland & Scottish Company immediately before nationalization (No. 10,000) plied up every weekday on the midday train from Derby: harbinger of a great change, which began in 1960 when the suburban service was turned over to diesel traction and the Type 4 'Peak' class locomotives appeared. By 1962 the steam engine had virtually gone.

*   *   *   *

Many millions of passengers have passed through St Pancras station during the past hundred years. Nearly all of them have taken it for granted, either regarding it simply as a place for catching a train to some destination north of London or, if they noticed the building at all, leaving their comments unrecorded. In spite of its obtrusive grandeur, it has figured very little in literature. No scenes have occurred in the Midland Grand Hotel like that in *The Belton Estate* set by Trollope in its humbler neighbour at King's Cross. No benevolent gentlemen with first-class tickets in their pockets are known to have found babies in the handbags deposited in its cloakroom; no addle-pated peers have sent telegrams from St Pancras to announce they were 'arriving tea time with landlady'. Even the great detectives, rushing over all England and half Europe in pursuit of their prey, have had little to do with this station. Sherlock Holmes avoided it almost pointedly. If he had to go into Derbyshire, in the affair of the Priory School, or into Bedfordshire, to look into the mystery of the Blanched Soldier at Tuxford Old Park, he travelled from Euston. M. Poirot, however, once ventured to St Pancras to take a northern express, stopped by special aristocratic privilege at Whimperley – shall we say in the West Riding of Yorkshire?[87]

The station makes a shadowy but memorable appearance in F. Anstey's *Vice Versa* (1882) as Mr Bultitude, seething with wrath, drives up in his cab and – seething still, obliged to pace up and down with the formidable Dr Grimstone – begins to feel 'an altogether novel sensation of utter insignificance upon that immense brown plain of platform and under the huge span of the arches whose girders were lost in wreaths of mingled fog and smoke'. Other writers have passed through it subsequently without comment. H G Wells arrived there, to begin his second assault on London, in 1888, lodging for one uncomfortable night in Judd Street and then in Theobald's Road.[88]

D H Lawrence must have used the station a good many times, travelling up and down to see his sister at Ripley; but he never has occasion to mention it.[89] Neither has Sir Osbert Sitwell in the four volumes of his autobiography, though Renishaw lies close to the old Midland line to the North and his father must surely have made many journeys up from Eckington station or Chesterfield.[90]

Is there, perhaps, once again something significant here? For all its size and imposing grandeur, the station soon came to be taken for granted. It was a point of arrival and departure, an instrument for its purpose, no more interesting to most passengers than the railway ticket that gave them admission to their train; part of the apparatus of London, nothing else.

There was one sort of journey, however, sometimes made from St Pancras that enlivened the station and made it conscious of itself. The Prince of Wales purchased the Sandringham estate just before his marriage in 1863; and on his frequent journeys there from London, he commonly used St Pancras station after the Tottenham and Hampstead line was opened in 1870.[91] It was much more conveniently situated for him than the Great Eastern stations, Shoreditch and Liverpool Street: not only nearer to Marlborough House and Buckingham Palace but outside the boundaries of the City of London, which could be crossed by a royal personage only with tiresome formality. In later years, protocol having eased a little and all regular working out of St Pancras on to the Great Eastern system having been discontinued, George V and his family used King's Cross or Liverpool Street for the purpose.

But royal journeys did not cease then altogether from St Pancras. When the Duke of Gloucester married and went to live at Barnwell in Northamptonshire in 1935, he travelled down to Kettering and the station was handsomely decorated. It lent itself ideally to occasions of this kind, with its grand entrance and wide carriage way along the platform; and when dressed for this purpose it looked much more brilliant than any other station in London.[92] At such moments it came into its own. It offered a glorious, spectacular setting for the arrival or departure of a king.

[1] The step had already been taken by some small companies, however. The Blyth & Tyne, for example, had decided to admit third-class passengers to all its trains in 1864: W W Tomlinson, *The North Eastern Railway* (1915), 660-1.

[2] See the useful tables in E Foxwell and T C Farrer, *Express Trains English and Foreign* (1889), 66, 165-78.

[3] For an illustration cf. J Simmons, *The Railways of Britain* (2nd ed., 1968), 235.

[4] G Behrend, *Pullman in Europe* (1962), 25-6; H Ellis, *Railway Carriages in the British Isles* (1965), 91-6.

[5] *The Times*, March 23, 1874, 9.

[6] Ellis, *Railway Carriages*, 68-71, 123; E L Ahrons, *Locomotive and Train Working* (1951-4), i.l.

[7] The Great Northern's time of $3\frac{3}{4}$ hours was not maintained: it was soon lengthened to 4 hours. A comparison between the two companies' service to Leeds is given in *Journal of the Royal Statistical Society* 47 (1884), 277.

[8] The timetables are given in Foxwell and Farrer, 10, 15. One wonders why, in a competition so spectacular, the Midland management did not run its 2 pm express *via* Leicester instead of Nottingham. This would have saved 11 miles and made it possible to bring the Midland train into Manchester at 6 o'clock or 6.5, ahead of both its rivals.

[9] M.P.I.C.E. 25 (1865-66), 285.

[10] C Dickens, *Dickens's Dictionary of London* (1879), 95-6.

[11] H P White, *A Regional History of the Railways of Great Britain: Greater London* (1963), 131.

[12] R B Fellows, *London to Cambridge by Train* (Cambridge, 1939), 14-15.

[13] G Raverat, *Period Piece* (1960 ed.), 93.

[14] W M Acworth, *The Railways of England* (5th ed., 1900), 158.

[15] I have not succeeded in discovering the exact date. The old arrangements, providing for the storage of a large number of carriages under the station roof, are shown clearly in Illustration 36. Evidently the alteration was made under authority given to the Traffic Committee in January, 1892, when £22,000 was voted for 'additional accommodation' at PRO St Pancras: RAIL 491/231, min. 7510. Platforms 3 and 4 were in use by 1893: *English Illustrated Magazine* 10 (1892-93), 659.

[16] August 17, 1891 (P.P. 1892, lxix, 209-12); August 12, 1894 (*ibid.*, 1895, lxxxvi, 204-12); May 17, 1901 (*ibid.*, 1901, lxvi, 455-9); September 3, 1906 (*ibid.*, 1907, lxxiv, 186-92).

[17] For a sober account see *The Times*, August 13, 1894, 4. The accidents produced a hullaballoo in some less responsible papers, which were reproved in *Railway Engineer* 15 (1894), 265.

[18] P.P. 1895, lxxxvi, 211.

[19] *Ibid.*, 1907, lxxiv, 191-2.

[20] *The Times*, October 16, 1967, 1.

[21] *Journal of the Royal Statistical Society* 46 (1883), 541.

[22] *Ibid.*, 563.

[23] *ibid.* 47 (1884), 277.

[24] Foxwell and Farrer, 51.

[25] PRO RAIL 491/21, min. 8511. The committee does not appear to have reported.

[26] Joshua Fielden of Todmorden at special meeting November 17, 1874 (RAIL 491/9).

[27] Foxwell and Farrer, 8.

[28] *The Railways of England* (1889), 167n, 169-70.

[29] Cf., for example, J T Burton-Alexander, *Railway Runs in Three Continents* (1900), 9, 11.

[30] PRO RAIL 491/740.

[31] *The Railways of England* (5th ed., 1900), 446. Acworth's phrase was something more than a rhetorical flourish, for the word was only just coming into use. It finds no place in the original *Oxford Dictionary* (letter D, 1897). It appears in the *Supplement* (1933), with

examples quoted from 1899 onwards. The earliest example of 'deceleration' given there is of 1897. All the examples of both words that are adduced from before 1920 relate to railways.

[32] *The Times,* July 2, 3, 4, 5, 6, 1901.

[33] *Railway Engineer* 23 (1902), 260.

[34] *Railway Engineer* 24 (1903), 105.

[35] In October 1958 – March 1961 I made 101 journeys between Leicester and St Pancras. Only 18 of these were punctual. On the other 83 the arrival was between 1 and 159 minutes late.

[36] It is amusing to note that this egregious sluggard among trains is one of the very few left in Britain today whose official title includes the word 'express'.

[37] *The Railways of England* (5th ed., 1900), 178-9.

[38] G Behrend, *Pullman in Europe* (1962), 39.

[39] The Midland Company ran the first true corridor train in Britain as early as 1874, but it proved unpopular: H Ellis, *Railway Carriages in the British Isles* (1965), 95. In the 'nineties it was slow to adopt the corridor train, preferring the internal vestibule without connection between one coach and the next (*ibid.,* 168); but the loss of seating space involved by this arrangement was virtually the same.

[40] *Ibid.,* 225.

[41] I am not forgetting Marylebone; but it hardly succeeded in establishing itself as one of the principal London stations.

[42] See Appendix One, pp 178-9.

[43] Making due allowance for an adjustment in the basis of the figures from 1902 onwards.

[44] PRO RAIL 491/1008-9.

[45] *Annual Register,* 1879, Chronicle, 3, 10.

[46] A L Bowley, *Prices and Wages in the United Kingdom, 1914-20* (1921), 165.

[47] PRO RAIL 491/9: 50th half-yearly meeting, February 2, 1869, 9.

[48] Ellis to W H Hodges, April 1, 1870: PRO RAIL 491/962, f.5. He repeated his inquiries about Spiers & Pond next year: same to same, February 16, 1871, f.10.

[49] PRO RAIL 491/9: 51st half-yearly meeting, August 18, 1869, 9.

[50] *Ibid.,* 62nd meeting, February 15, 1875, 4.

[51] *Ibid.,* 63rd meeting, August 17, 1875, 7.

[52] *Ibid.,* 68th meeting, February 19, 1878, 7.

[53] *Ibid.,* 70th meeting, February 18, 1879, 3.

[54] *Ibid.,* 91st meeting, August 9, 1889, 4-5.

[55] PRO RAIL 491/282, min 1787.

[56] *Ibid.,* min 1813.

[57] *Ibid.,* mins. 1935, 1957.

[58] *Ibid.,* RAIL 491/275, mins. 46,58.

[59] Oliver Carter, *An Illustrated History of British Railway Hotels 1838-1983* (1990), 86-87.

[60] C Dickens, *Dickens's Dictionary of London* (1879), 117.

[61] C Dickens, *Dickens's Dictionary of London* (1879), 224,83.

[62] *Caterer and Hotel-Keepers' Gazette,* 16 December 1901, 521; ibid., 15 February 1904, 53.

[63] Baedeker, *London* (1911), 7.

[64] F Muirhead (ed.), *London and its Environs* (1918), 13, 14.

[65] Baedeker, *London* (1930), 9.

[66] *Times,* 26 April 1892, 6; Gavin Stamp, *An Architect of Promise* (Donington, Lincs., 2002), 341.

[67] E A Pratt, *British Railways and the Great War* (1921), 457-8.

[68] Sir A Webb (ed.), *London of the Future* (1921), 76, 78.

[69] By an odd chance, this drastic reduction in the Scottish services from St Pancras coincided with the appearance of a phrase that led to some delicious misunderstandings. In the musical comedy *Funny Face* in 1928 Sydney Howard cried out tipsily 'St George for England!' , to be met with Leslie Henson's retort 'St Pancras for Scotland!' This led a correspondent of *Notes & Queries* to inquire solemnly in 1935: 'What had the Roman boy-martyr, about whom we know so little, to do with Scotland?' Other correspondents then pointed out that the reference was to the station (168 *Notes & Queries* (1935), 315, 374, 410). But Professor Meeks was also misled by it – more pardonably, on the far side of the Atlantic. 'The station,' he says, ' is the chief one for trains to the Highlands [it never was that, even in the most expansive days of the Midland]; there is a saying in London, "St George for England, St Pancras for Scotland"' (*The Railway Station*, 96n).

[70] It was more evenly spread through the day and included a fast train as late as 9.30 pm, whereas the last left King's Cross at 7.10.

[71] The comparable service from Marylebone comprised eight trains taking an average of 121 minutes; only one of them came up to the *average* of the trains from St Pancras.

[72] G C Nash, *The L.M.S. at War* (1946), 45.

[73] R Bell, *History of the British Railways during the War, 1939-45* (1946), 192-3; PRO: Bomb Census Returns HO 198/31.

[74] *Railway Gazette* 109 (1958), 553.

[75] J H Forshaw and P Abercrombie, *County of London Plan* (1943), 69.

[76] *Administrative County of London Development Plan 1951*: Analysis (1951), para. 871.

[77] *Railway Gazette* 87 (1947), 142.

[78] *ibid.* 107 (1957), 679-82.

[79] *ibid.* 103 (1955), 235.

[80] See his *Wanderings in London* (1951), 153.

[81] *Railway Gazette* 105 (1956), 392, 419.

[82] *Railway Magazine* 103 (1957), 80.

[83] *ibid.* 105 (1959), 812.

[84] *Railway Gazette* 119 (1963), 34.

[85] It was under Johnson that the famous red livery was adopted for the Midland Company's locomotives, in place of the former green; the first experiment with it took place in 1883. The standard of finish he insisted on was almost incredibly high. Each engine received seven coats of paint – two of lead grey, four of purple brown, and then a top coat of crimson lake with purple brown mixed into it – followed by five coats of varnish. When one of his machines was to be sent out for exhibition, the underside of the boiler barrel was painted cream, to throw light on the motion below. (Ellis, *The Midland Railway*, 82-3.)

[86] *Bulletin of the International Railway Congress* 12 (Brussels, 1898), 148.

[87] Agatha Christie, 'Dead Man's Mirror': *Murder in the Mews* (1937).

[88] H G Wells, *Experiment in Autobiography* (1937 ed.), i. 312. He had travelled up from Etruria in the Potteries. One wonders why he had not gone to Euston.

[89] 'The huge arch of the station' is, however, referred to at the close of chap. v of *Women in Love*.

[90] Jack Simmons seems to have overlooked one of the most poignant moments in twentieth-century literature, the final leave-taking at St. Pancras in August 1915 between Vera Brittain and Roland Leighton: *Testament of Youth* (1933, repr. 1978), 188-9.

[91] Williams, *Midland Railway*, 353.

[92] See, for example, the dazzling photograph of the eastern gateway dressed for the departure of Queen Elizabeth II and the Duke of Edinburgh for Sudbury, Staffs., in 1957: *Railway Gazette* 106 (1957), 439. Unfortunately no print of this picture is available for reproduction.

CHAPTER V

Controversy

Ever since it was first planned, more than a century ago, St Pancras station has been a centre of controversy: over the eviction of the previous occupants of the site, with the unhappy occupants them-selves and the social reformers who championed them; over the treatment of the St Pancras churchyard; among the shareholders about the enormous cost of the building as it made its slow way towards completion; in our own time, about its continued use as a railway station. But the great-est, the most long drawn-out controversy of all has been aroused by the building itself, more especially by Scott's hotel. This is an argument about architecture, about questions of taste.

It began while the building was still being erected, before any part of the hotel was in use, in the staid *Quarterly Review*. Its number for April 1872 included a critique of several books on architecture, among them Eastlake's *History of the Gothic Revival*, comprising, almost from start to finish, a fierce assault on contemporary architects and their practice in organizing their work, based on a quite fanciful notion of the part played by masons in medieval building. The critic's most savage assault was directed against Scott; and what he has to say about the St Pancras hotel epitomizes so com-pletely the case that can be made against it that it deserves quotation in full:

'About the Midland Railway Terminus . . .there are not two opinions.
Here the public taste has been exactly suited, and every kind of architec-tural decoration has been made thoroughly common and unclean. The building inside and out is covered with ornament, and there is polished marble enough to furnish a Cathedral. The very parapet of the cab road is panelled and perforated, at a cost that would have supplied foot-warmers to all the trains for years to come. This monument of confectionery is a fair specimen of the result of competition among architects for the approval of judges whom they know to be incompetent. The "Midland" directors are able administrators of the railway business, and probably of their own; but was there any evidence that they were qualified in any way to decide

upon the respective merits of the competitors, or to select a design to be built in an important Metropolitan thoroughfare? Is any one of these gentlemen furnished with the necessary knowledge? And if not, how can their accumulated ignorance become efficient in its stead? These are questions that – in the interests of the art, about which they are so very careful when their own interests are equally involved – the competing architects ought, as a condition precedent, to have had satisfactorily answered. Judging by the building, however, we imagine that quite a different course was pursued; and in the successful design, at any rate, the noble art of building has been treated as a mere trade advertisement. Showy and expensive, it will, for the present, be a striking contrast with its adjoining neighbour. The Great Northern Terminus is not graceful, but it is simple, characteristic, and true. No one would mistake its nature and use. The Midland front is inconsistent in style, and meretricious in detail; a piece of common "art manufacture" that makes the Great Northern front appear by contrast positively charming. There is no relief or quiet in any part of the work. The eye is constantly troubled and tormented, and the mechanical patterns follow one another with such rapidity and perseverance, that the mind becomes irritated where it ought to be gratified, and goaded to criticism where it should be led calmly to approve. There is here a complete travesty of noble associations, and not the slightest care to save these from a sordid contact. An elaboration that might be suitable for a Chapter-house, or a Cathedral choir, is used as an "advertising medium" for bagmen's bedrooms and the costly discomforts of a terminus hotel, and the architect is thus a mere expensive rival of the company's head cook, in catering for the low enjoyments of the great travelling crowd. To be consistent, the directors should not confine their expression of artistic feeling to these great buildings only. Their porters might be dressed as javelin men, their guards as beefeaters, and their station-masters don the picturesque attire of Garter-king-at-arms. Their carriages might be copied from the Lord Mayor's show, and even the engine wheels might imitate the Gothic window near their terminus at York. These things, however, will eventually come; the water tank, we see, is moulded in the Gothic style.

'Yet who is to blame for all this? The directors meant well, no doubt, and are in a state of childish or other ignorance. And if the architect is held responsible, he may refer at once to the system. Of course the work is mechanical and unimaginative; but does the public demand anything better? Are there those among us, who are able to judge of work and to sympathize with and efficiently to support a genuine workman? We have, in fact, no real artist workmen, like Fischer of Nuremberg, or John of Padua, and our enterprising directors must, therefore, put up with what they can get – an eminent architect, "art manufacture", and sufficient money.'[1]

This remarkable tirade not unnaturally gave great offence. As his *Recollections* show, Scott was a man of more than ordinary self-esteem; but even someone more modest would have been deeply affronted by it. The critic preserved his anonymity, leaving everybody to guess who he was. On the quite unfounded suspicion that the article had been written by his former pupil Thomas Graham Jackson, Scott ceased cordial relations with him for the rest of his life.[2] He had begun to write his memoirs in 1864, and had laid them aside uncompleted. He resumed them in July 1872,[3] and an attentive reader of them is bound to feel that he did so, in part at least, to vindicate himself against the monstrous calumnies he had been subjected to in the *Quarterly* three months earlier.[4]

Other people were outraged besides Scott. The *Architect* dismissed the *Quarterly* critic as 'an able wordmonger' and advised him to try his hand at the business of designing a building to learn what difficulties it involved.[5] The *Edinburgh Review*, as always the chief rival of the *Quarterly*, carried a scathing reply to the indictment in 1875.[6]

This was not the only adverse opinion expressed on the work at the time. James Fergusson, in the second edition of his powerful *History of Modern Architecture*, published in 1873, was far from flattering to it:

'If the Great Northern station is a success, it is because it is simply an unaffected piece of engineering skill, and makes no pretensions to be an object of architectural art. The same, however, cannot be said of its more ambitious neighbour at St Pancras, on which so much ornament has been bestowed that it is elevated unmistakably into the higher class, though the mode in which this has been done renders it doubtful whether it is either so pleasing or so successful as its plainer sister. As an engineering *tour de force*, the roof of its great shed is as yet unrivalled. It is 700 feet long by 200 feet clear span, without an apparent tie of any sort. The ties, in fact, are the beams that form the roof of the vaults below and support the floor of the station. Add to these dimension, that it is 100 feet high, and it becomes colossal in every respect. But was it worth while to encounter all the engineering difficulties, and go to such an expense to attain this result? Had it been divided by a range of two columns into two halls, each 120 feet wide, it would have been equally convenient, would have cost less, and looked both longer and wider and higher that the present one.[7] As it is, it kills everything; the carriages and engines look like toy trains, and human beings like ants. There is no proportion between the shed and its uses, and everything looks out of place, and most of all the Gothic mouldings and brickwork, borrowed from the domestic architecture of the Middle Ages, which with its pretty littlenesses thrusts itself between the gigantic iron ribs of the roof. Add to all this the curious clumsiness of the medieval timbering of the roof of the booking-office, in daring contrast with all the refinements of nineteenth-century construction in the neighbouring shed, and you have the two systems in such violent contrast that it is quite evident that this is not the direction on which it is possible an amalgamation can ever by effected. We may regret the plainness of the Great Northern station, but it is better it should remain as it is, rather than that it should be disfigured with incongruous medievalism like the station of the Midland Railway, which stands next to it.'[8]

Where pundits led, other men felt entitled to follow. Augustus Hare, for example, inserted into the sixth edition of his *Walks in London* a gratuitous reference to 'the Midland Terminus Hotel, Scott's tawdry masterpiece'.[9]

Some of those who admired the building were puzzled by the meagre impact that it apparently made. 'It has not yet seemed to produce any great effect upon the public mind', complained the *Architect* in 1872, 'and we confess to some feeling of disappointment at the small amount of attention which has been paid to so fine a work. The tower especially is a striking and picturesque object, and all the patterns and the details of the masonry are full of beauty.'[10]

There are perhaps two reasons why St Pancras achieved less *éclat* than might seem to be owing to its size and grandeur. First, it was a very long time under way. The plans were published, and discussed in the technical press, in 1867. The train-shed drew public attention frequently while it was being built. When the station was brought into use there seemed nothing more to be said, and the event passed almost unnoticed. The hotel was erected so gradually, stage by stage, that it too slipped into use quite silently. No part of the building was inaugurated with any formal opening ceremony. There was no single event, therefore, to elicit considered critical comment.

The second reason is that, though the St Pancras hotel was large and splendid, it did not stand alone. It was one of the series of international hotels that began with the Grosvenor and the Langham and was continued with a group around Charing Cross – those in Northumberland Avenue from 1878 onwards, the Cecil in the Strand. Each of them outstripped its predecessors and competitors; when the Cecil began life in 1886 it was, with its 800 rooms, the largest hotel in Europe.[11] Each was a nine days' wonder and then fell back to become an accepted part of London life. The St Pancras hotel could expect no more attention than this; through the hesitancy of its inauguration it received less.

As a building, however, St Pancras received much conventional admiration in the late nineteenth century. *The Times* observed in a leading article when Scott died that 'the architect of a railway station does not generally aim very high, but Sir Gilbert Scott certainly produced in the Midland station at St Pancras the most beautiful terminus in London, remarkable alike for its convenience and its inspiring effect'.[12] The writers of books about London usually commended it. It was 'the noblest of all the structures of this kind in London', observed one in 1887;[13] 'it stands without rival for palatial beauty, comfort, and convenience', wrote another ten years later.[14] Seldom did any one express his admiration for it with passion. But one journalist, in the course of a tour of the London railway stations in 1893, authentically caught a little of its magic:

> 'Go at night to St Pancras . . .at an hour when no trains are leaving. Walk along No. 3 platform as far as the first seat and then look back. If you are fortunate enough to catch a grouping of the sort indicated in the illustration[15] – a hidden engine belching out clouds of steam that mingle with the fog overhead – it does not need a very powerful imagination to fancy you are in some great temple. The white clouds come from the altar fire; above it, half lost in vapour, is the great clock, its huge round dial like the face of a monstrous idol before which burn in solemn stillness the hanging lamps gleaming silver and violet and rose.'[16]

*   *   *   *

The influence of St Pancras on railway engineering and architecture was considerable, but very uneven. In London it was the last of its line. No other train-shed there repeated its pattern or made any attempt to vie with it in size. The next large terminal station to be built was Liverpool Street, and that was treated in an entirely different way. Holborn Viaduct and Marylebone were both modest in scale; and in the very big new buildings of the early twentieth century, the reconstructed Victoria (Brighton side) and Waterloo, the roof was horizontal, the curving iron ribs of St Pancras giving place to girders of steel.

Only three more railway hotels were to come in London: Liverpool Street (1875-84), Holborn Viaduct (1877), and Marylebone (1899). At Liverpool Street station the Great Eastern Railway employed no architect; Edward Wilson, the Company's Engineer, was responsible for the whole building.[17] It is an indication of the emergence of architecture as a fully-recognized profession that the failure to employ an architect on this work was made a matter of public criticism. An anonymous correspondent delivered himself thus to the Editor of the *Builder* :

'I am not an architect, and have very little reason to write on architectural subjects, but I have ... a most sincere respect and admiration for masters of the craft, ... and when I see a great work lacking this foresight and skill, and find, as appearances would lead one to infer, that no architect has been employed, – only an engineer, – I cannot forbear bringing it under the notice of one who, like you, is charged with the public duty of rebuking great defects in building, as much as of encouraging merit'[18]

The hotel was designed to be fitted into the façade that Wilson had already supplied, by C E Barry (nephew of the architect of Charing Cross and Cannon Street). It was opened, after long delays, at the end of May, 1884.[19]

The Great Eastern Hotel at Liverpool Street was managed and worked by the Company itself. Different arrangements were adopted for its two successors. The architect of the London Chatham & Dover Company's station at Holborn Viaduct was Lewis H Isaacs, who gave a comic account of the casual way in which he was invited to undertake the work when a party of visitors from the Architectural Association was being shown the building, during its construction, in 1876:

'Mr Forbes, the Chairman of the railway company, said to him: "We are going to build a station on the Holborn Viaduct; if you like to undertake its design we shall be happy to engage you. For the disposition of the lines and the lower part of the building I must refer you to Mr Mills, the Company's Engineer. You will have to provide a restaurant, and that may develop into an hotel, and you must also allow for circumstances if the Company ultimately remove their headquarters from Victoria to Holborn"'[20]

The railway company evidently had not much interest in the hotel for its own sake. It was let on advantageous terms to the catering firm of Spiers & Pond and opened, three and a half years after the station, on November 17, 1877.[21]

When the Manchester Sheffield & Lincolnshire Company planned its extension to London in the 'nineties, it envisaged the construction of an hotel between its terminus and the Marylebone Road. The cost of the whole project was so large, however, that it had to content itself with leasing the site to a consortium headed by Sir Blundell Maple, on condition that the Company should have the option of purchasing the hotel at some future date. The option was never exercised.[22]

The Hotel Great Central (or Grand Central, as it was called at first)[23] differed from St Pancras not merely in style – its architect, Col. R W Edis, adopted the Jacobean fashionable at the turn of the century – but also in its position: quite detached from Marylebone station, to which it was linked by an awning of iron and glass. If it did not rival St Pancras in size, the new hotel competed for custom from the same towns in the Midlands. Built more than twenty years later, the Hotel Great Central naturally enjoyed some amenities that were not to be found at the rival establishment: a cycle track on the roof, for example, to enable pursy business men to reduce their weight.[24] It defeats the imagination to think how *that* could have been provided among Scott's Gothic pinnacles and chimneys. But as the history of its construction shows, railway companies no longer felt the same conviction about the value of these huge London hotels as they had felt in the 'fifties and 'sixties. That at Marylebone was the last.

It must therefore be said that the influence of St Pancras in London was slight. It was stronger outside: in Glasgow, in Lancashire, in America and ultimately in India.

In the 1860s the main stations of Glasgow were a disgrace to the city. (One of them, Buchanan Street, survived, little altered, until 1966, by which time it was easily one of the most abominable in Western Europe.) Improvement was slow to come, and when it did it was due first to the smallest of the three main railways serving the city, the Glasgow & South Western. This company, struggling perpetually with its larger rival the Caledonian, entered into an alliance with the Midland, based upon the building of the Midland's line across the Pennines from Settle to Carlisle, where the two railways would meet. That brave project had been authorized in the ominous summer of 1866. It had been widely expected to lead to an amalgamation of the two companies, and three times – in 1867, 1872 and 1873 – their shareholders approved Bills to this end, only to see them rejected by Parliament. The building of the line over the Pennines went ahead none the less; and when it was completed through trains began to run from St Pancras, on May 1, 1876.

The passengers arrived in Glasgow at a brand new station, and what they saw was a modified copy of the station they had left in London. The buildings were designed by Thomas Willson,[25] the roof by R M Ordish. It was a copy in that its plan was the same, the train-shed covered with an iron and glass roof made in a single span, an hotel in front raised up above St Enoch Square as St Pancras was raised above the Euston Road. It was modified in that the roof was narrower – 200 feet against 240 feet; its structure was different, for there were no underground vaults; and the Venetial Gothic brickwork had given place to Scottish Baronial in stone. The contractors for the roof at St Enoch were not the Butterley Company but their neighbours Andrew Handyside & Co. of Derby. The station was recognized at once as setting a quite new standard in Glasgow. Of the rest of the stations there the *Builder* remarked very temperately that 'they can be described as little better than vast wooden sheds'.[26]

Train-sheds comparable with that of St Pancras were also erected at Liverpool (Central) in 1874 and at Manchester (Central) six years later. John Fowler designed the one at Liverpool, which was 169 feet wide, with the bow-string truss that he had used in the Chatham Station at Victoria. The shed at the Manchester station (also constructed by Handyside & Co.) was 210 feet wide and adhered closely to the St Pancras model, except that it was segmental in shape, not pointed. Neither of these stations included an hotel. The site of the one at Liverpool forbade anything of the kind, without the very expensive diversion of Ranelagh Street. The possibility of an hotel was envisaged at Manchester (Central), and the offices for the reception of passengers at the front were accordingly built in the cheapest possible manner, of wood. When the hotel was at length constructed, by the Midland Company, in 1898-1903, it was on a more commodious site opposite, looking on to St Peter's Square.[27] The temporary wooden offices then became permanent in their squalid inadequacy: a standing reproach to their owners and to the city of Manchester.

Though none of these three stations belonged to the Midland Railway itself,[28] they were built by companies closely connected with it; they were in fact the termini in the largest cities to which the Midland ran express trains from London. By strange fate, all three were closed in the 1960s: Glasgow (St Enoch) and Liverpool (Central) were later demolished but Manchester (Central) survived to be reopened as an exhibition centre in 1986. Remembering that St Pancras also came under threat in 1966, it might be wondered whether the 'St Pancras pattern' was fundamentally faulty, or extravagantly expensive to maintain. That was not in fact the reason for the closure of the counterparts to St Pancras in other cities. Those stations were shut because it became possible with railway nationalisation to concentrate services which were hitherto operated by different companies.

St Pancras was not much imitated on the Continent. The splendid Anhalt station in Berlin (begun in 1872) owed a little to it; so did the vast roofs, in multiple spans, of the main stations at Frankfurt and Dresden.[29] The Americans, on the other hand, took St Pancras to their hearts.

To Commodore Vanderbilt St Pancras, with its monumental predecessors and contemporaries in Europe, represented a challenge to the United States, which had no station anywhere that could be put into competition with them.[30] The new Grand Central station in New York, for the use of his companies, was begun in the year after the opening of St Pancras and completed in 1871. Vanderbilt instructed his architect, I C Buckhout, that it was to be the largest station in the world.[31] His orders were obeyed. Its area was five acres, as against the four and a half of St Pancras. The train-shed was remarkably like Barlow's; its arches too were tied below the tracks. The American roof, however, was smaller: the same height, but only 200 feet wide and 600 feet long – covering 13,300 square yards as against the 18,800 square yards of St Pancras. The plan and external treatment were quite different. When it was new, it was one of the principal sights of North America.[32] St Pancras was again imitated at the Park Square station in Boston in 1872 – in one respect more exactly, for the roof here was not segmental but pointed.[33] The St Pancras span remained unsurpassed until the Pennsylvania Railroad built its Jersey City station, which was 10 feet wider, in 1888.[34] The same company won the competition outright with the Broad Street station in Philadelphia, whose roof had a span of 300 feet 8 inches, which has never been equalled in any station building since. The exterior of that station also distinctly echoes St Pancras, though on a confined and unimpressive site, in a different idiom, and with none of Scott's extravagant ebullience.[35]

But perhaps the real successor to St Pancras was not in America, but in India. The Victoria Terminus, Bombay, was conceived of two years after St Pancras was finished, and was announced to the world in a magnificent water-colour by Axel Haig exhibited at the Royal Academy in 1880 *(plate X)*. Its architect F W Stevens blended Scott's Venetian Gothic with Indian styles, stretched over a 300 ft. long façade, and surmounted by a dome carrying a sculpture representing progress. This 'St Pancras of the Orient' was meant to be completed in 1887 to celebrate Queen Victoria's Jubilee, but in fact was not finished till 1896 by which time such extravagance seemed, in Britain at least, increasingly outmoded.[36]

* * * *

It was just that quality of extravagance, of completely confident self-assertion realized in an intensely romantic form, that offended the *Quarterly* reviewer and James Fergusson. As the nineteenth century wore into the twentieth, the mid-Victorian age began to be seen in a new light. Both the certainty and the idealism that it represented were becoming tarnished. The men of the 'nineties and the Edwardians poked fun at their mid-Victorian forebears: quiet fun, behind their hands, but sardonic fun too, for they were uneasily aware that their own achievement was on a smaller scale, less likely to last, that the power and consequence of their country was declining.

A building like St Pancras station, which embodied so accurately the achievement of the age just past, was bound to fall into disfavour. Some people could still look at it without passion and commend it strictly on its own merits. In 1913 Martin Briggs found it 'typical of Sir Gilbert Scott in his happiest vein, one of the greatest works of the Gothic Revival . . . [It] possesses a freshness usually lacking in buildings of its age . . .No important English station of the nineteenth century surpasses St Pancras in general excellence'.[37] More usually, however, it was ignored, or mildly vilified.

The full reaction against the Victorians set in after the First World War, which had evidently destroyed so much of what they had stood for. Lytton Strachey raised peals of fun at Gilbert Scott's expense in his *Queen Victoria*. Kenneth Clark raised more in a book published in 1928 that started out from the proposition that 'the real reason why the Gothic Revival has been neglected is that it produced so little on which our eyes can rest without pain'.[38] It is here, too, that we discern again the legend that the St Pancras hotel was a re-worked version of the rejected designs for the Foreign Office.[39]

In the 'twenties and 'thirties Scott's reputation sank to its lowest depths, and St Pancras sank with it. Reilly treated them both with silent contempt.[40] A E Richardson, in a diatribe peppered with inaccuracy, was patronizing. Under him the Palmerston myth reaches its final form – 'Lord Palmerston rejected *this identical conception* [41] when it was presented in its first state as a design for the Foreign Office'. He goes on: 'Yet viewed in all the glory of the Euston Road it has a strange attraction, its Hartz mountain top scenery and pinnacled summits point the moral of an active and prosperous career' *(ill. 47)*. Richardson never allied himself with the modernist movement in architecture, but like the most fervent followers of that movement, he believed that the pure engineering aesthetic of the train shed should be freed from its association with Scott's architecture: 'How fine St Pancras Le Vault would look if Lord Stamp would consent to the removal of the expensive Gothic hotel now almost derelict.'[42]

Lord Stamp, President of the London Midland & Scottish Railway, contributed to the discussion that followed this paper. His words are highly characteristic, of him and of all he stood for:

> 'I always commiserate with my friends in the architectural profession when I think of the contrast between their art and that, we will say, of the great violinist or vocalist, rendering something which in quality is really immortal and ought to be enjoyed by all ages, but in a medium which is gone at once, whereas the architect expresses an idea which will be laughed at in twenty years' time in something which is imperishable, so that the chairman of a railway company finds on his hands St Pancras station! When I feel inclined to be at all positive on the subject of architecture, I turn up the contemporary accounts of that station and the enraptured way in which it was received as the newest and greatest note in the adaptation of Gothic architecture to modern industrial life, and then I reflect that today I could

47. The Midland Grand in Euston Road in 1926.

not even get rid of the sculptured caps to the architects of Liverpool cathedral.[43] Moreover, it is impossible to put in a new piece of heating apparatus or anything of that kind without meeting with the same obstacles that would be encountered in modifying the Rock of Gibraltar.'[44]

There are two elements here. The coarse-grained philistinism is all that we should expect of Lord Stamp, then busily engaged in compassing the destruction of Euston. The last sentence, however, is plain common sense, and it must arouse our sympathy. It refers obliquely to the closing of the hotel four years earlier and to the formidable problem of finding an alternative use for the building.

*   *   *   *

In 1935 – the year in which the Midland Grand Hotel was closed – the London Midland & Scottish Company announced its plans for the complete rebuilding of Euston Station. It was a very big scheme, though it was confined to rebuilding and did not provide for the electrification that was undertaken in the 1960s. As soon as these plans were published, rumours began to circulate that one consequence of implementing them would be the closing of St Pancras. These were premature. No decision had in fact been taken. The question was – and is – very far from a simple one. Even if Euston could be made capable of taking the traffic of St Pancras as well as its own, complex problems of routeing were involved. Trains from Leicester and stations northward could travel easily enough by way of the line of the old Midland Counties Railway from Wigston to Rugby or by that from Market Harborough to Northampton. From Kettering and Wellingborough, the line along the Nene Valley could be used to Blisworth, but this meant bypassing the main station in Northampton, or else running into it and reversing. For trains from stations south of Wellingborough there was no satisfactory alternative to the Midland line, though such could be made by the building of new junctions – at Harlesden, for example, taking traffic from the Midland at Brent. Or there was the possibility of diverting all this outer suburban traffic into the tunnel below St Pancras station, to run by the Metropolitan 'widened lines' into Moorgate.

By one or more of these expedients the problem presented by passenger traffic might be solved. None of them, however, provided an adequate means of coping with the goods traffic that was really more important: the coal that was still being delivered in great quantities at Cambridge Street, the miscellaneous freight handled at St Pancras and Somers Town goods stations.

The Euston scheme of 1935 was never implemented. During the Second World War itself new ideas began to emerge, from the much more radical re-thinking of transport problems that sprang partly from the bombing of London and partly from long-term economic and social changes that were evidently on their way. An architects' reconstruction committee, for example, put forward a plan in 1943 for the reduction of all the London terminal stations to four, with Euston, St Pancras, and King's Cross merged into a single station on two levels.[45]

Where the railways were concerned, all such distant planning was made more difficult for the moment – though in the long run easier – by the nationalization of 1947. This necessarily entailed great changes in their administration, which had to be carried through at a time of economic stringency, to the accompaniment of noisy and conflicting political comment. In the first phase of their history, from 1947 to 1955, British Railways were forced to devote their main energies to the establishment of the new organization. They were already looking forward to the future, however; and with the Modernization Plan of 1955 they began to move towards it. That Plan provided for the electrification of the main line out of Euston as well as for the long-delayed reconstruction of Euston station itself, on lines quite different from those laid down twenty years earlier. This time the plan was carried into effect: moving more slowly than its authors hoped, but still steadily, until the electrification was completed in 1967. The re-building of Euston involved the demolition of Philip Hardwick's great Doric arch in 1962, despite a vigorous campaign to keep it which went as far as a deputation to the Prime Minister, Harold Macmillan.[46] While the work was in progress, St Pancras became busier than before, with the Manchester traffic switched from Euston. A good deal of money was spent on the station and its equipment in 1956-63.[47]

The first report by Richard (later Lord) Beeching on the reorganisation of the railways appeared in 1963. In it, the Midland line to London made a respectable figure in passenger traffic, whilst from Kettering southward it carried about as much freight as the Euston line and more than that to King's Cross. As far as passenger services were concerned, the Report proposed no more than the closure of wayside stations north of Kettering.[48] The second Beeching Report, however, which was issued in February 1965, told a different tale. There it was announced[49] that the 'route selected for development' for traffic to London from the Midland system north of Leicester would be that from Leicester to Nuneaton, where it joined the electrified trunk line from the North to Euston. Though it was not specifically proposed to shut down all the lines not 'selected for development' – that would have meant that sizeable towns like Blackpool, Worcester, and Cambridge would have been deprived entirely of railway services – there would clearly, under this plan, be small future for a line 100 miles long, running parallel with others, like that from Leicester to St Pancras. By 1984 – which was the ominous date chosen for the complete realization of this prophecy – it would evidently have disappeared.

Two years later, under different political pressures, the policy of the Railways Board had changed. The old Midland line was restored to the 'network for development'. But by that time it had become known that, whatever might happen to the line, the Board intended to amalgamate St Pancras with King's Cross.

The news of this plan broke on August 25, 1966. On that day it was announced by British Railways that they intended to amalgamate the two stations 'to create a single modern terminus'. An outline plan of the proposal was to be sent to the Minister of Transport 'as soon as possible', though at an unspecified date; the cost of the operation was unknown. Even if it was 'hoped' that the roof of St Pancras could be incorporated into the new station, it was 'likely that only fragments of the original buildings would be recognizable'.[50]

The public response to this announcement was complex and varied. Professor Nikolaus Pevsner, writing as Chairman of the Victorian Society, gave an immediate warning against allowing any unnecessary demolition – like that perpetrated at Euston, which had occurred simply 'because those in power were too ignorant and too callous'. He went on:

> 'What one has a right and indeed a duty to demand is an awareness of
> the high values at stake among those laying down the terms of reference
> for the new building. The terminal building at St Pancras, I would think,
> can certainly be saved, as it is independent of the station itself. The train
> shed might be incorporated also, if the designers think hard enough. King's
> Cross may be more problematic.'[51]

Professor Pevsner then went on to adduce the parallel of the central station in Rome – 'a masterpiece of modern architecture, not in spite of the fact that it has to preserve a substantial piece of ancient building, but partly because that preservation was part of the programme' – and to call for imagination and thought of the same order here.

The architectural correspondent of *The Times*, in a temperate survey, argued that 'though either station, if demolished or substantially altered, would be a very great loss, St Pancras would be the greater' on account of its 'visual richness and excitement'. He concluded that the whole task would demand 'the initiative as well as the co-operation of the planning authority' – implying clearly enough that no solution to the problem ought to be accepted unless it had been worked out by British Railways and that authority in partnership.[52]

A flood of comment was now released, swelling the correspondence columns of *The Times* for the next fortnight. It began with a robust denunciation of St Pancras from Sir Edward Playfair, writing as 'one who positively loathes the building' and who believes in 'the virtues of demolition'.[53] He found no one to follow him, though Professor Michael Howard was willing to suspend judgment until the new plans were published, preferring in the meanwhile to 'keep hold of nurse for fear of finding something worse'.[54] Two or three correspondents were prepared to sacrifice the hotel if the station could be kept: among them Mr J L F Wright, Vice-Chairman of the Butterley Company.[55]

But the general trend of opinion, as expressed here, was plain: that the building should be preserved as a whole. Professor Hondelink argued, from a strictly functional point of view, that the precedent set at Euston, where the plan had been 'both ambitious and amateurish', should not be followed, since there were 'no valid reasons, operational or economic, for the replacement' of the two stations.[56] Another correspondent, who used St Pancras ten times a week, said he seldom looked at it but found it entirely convenient for every purpose he required. 'St Pancras *works*,' he concluded: 'leave it alone.'[57] From an aesthetic point of view, one writer praised the brickwork, seeing the station as 'truly a masterpiece of craft if not always accepted as art'.[58] Mr Eric de Maré, having indicated his contempt for Sir Edward Playfair's 'facetious tone', summed up his own view – and many other people's – pungently:

> 'Whatever one may feel about St Pancras as a work of art, no one can deny that its presence is powerful, not least as a grand symbol of what, for all its faults, was one of the greatest periods in this island's history. As a callow architectural student I despised all Victorian architecture; having photographed it extensively, and so studied it closely, for many years, I can now see those many virtues it contains which are so signally lacking in the impersonal, faceless, joyless, minimal, rent-raising erections of today – not least at St Pancras.'[59]

The Times correspondence did not stand alone; but it affords a good indication of opinion. As it closed, the paper published a reproduction of O'Connor's painting of the building seen from the Pentonville Road in 1881 *(plate IX)*.[60]

There, for the moment, the matter rested, while British Railways matured their plans. In the following summer the working party charged with the task (which included representatives of the Ministry of Housing and Local Government, the Greater London Council, and the Borough Councils of Camden and Islington) completed an interim report. This envisaged the retention of the façade of King's Cross, with a new station behind it, and the closing of St Pancras. The train-shed, it urged, 'could become a sportsdrome with an indoor running track, football pitch and tennis courts. Alternatively or in addition, there could be an exhibition hall.' No pronouncement was offered at this stage on the fate of the former hotel.[61]

The final report followed in September. It recommended the closure of St Pancras, with the services from the old Midland system diverted. Expresses from Leicester and stations northward would run by a newly-electrified line to Nuneaton and so to Euston; other trains would take the old line from Leicester and Bedford to Moorgate. The notion that the train-shed at St Pancras might become a sports centre or exhibition hall was endorsed. Nothing was said of the hotel. The whole scheme was to cost £8½ million. A sketch of the proposals as they affected King's Cross evoked a terse and withering comment from the architectural correspondent of the *Daily Telegraph*.[62]

The Ministry of Housing was represented on that committee. It had two interests in the matter, which were to some extent in conflict. One argument in favour of demolishing St Pancras station was that it would free land that would be valuable for housing. On the other hand the same Ministry was also responsible for the preservation of historic buildings, and in the previous December Lord Kennet, its Parliamentary Secretary, had given an undertaking that it would not allow the station to be demolished 'unless convinced that preservation was incompatible with imperative operational requirements and that there was no possible alternative use for the building.'[63] There was one odd feature in this statement. At that time the building enjoyed no protection under the Ancient Monuments or Planning Acts; its demolition would not therefore have required the Minister's consent. On November 2, 1967, however, the position altered, when the Minister announced that he had made an order putting the train-shed and hotel into Grade I of the list of buildings of 'special architectural or historic interest'.[64]

By this time it was abundantly evident that taste had changed. The building had come to be praised again, with a new fervour. Its uncompromising romanticism began to evoke a vehement, though sometimes slightly wry, admiration. Mr Richard Buckle tells us of taking the French artist André Beaurepaire to see it in 1947, and of the extravagant fantasy it inspired in him: 'As we stood in awe before it, uttering groans like those of a dying man, he saw it as the lair of one of his imaginary heroines, a fierce and beautiful vampire called Lady Blue.'[65] His pen and ink sketches of the building catch some of its moods and qualities admirably. Mr Betjeman praised its grandeur, though by no means uncritically. 'A station apart', he called it, 'a Royal Station', adding prophetically: 'I have little doubt that British Railways will do away with St Pancras altogether. It is too beautiful and too romantic to survive. It is not of this age.'[66] Mr Boase saw in it 'a Gothic design of splendid intricacy, which should be in every way ill suited for its purpose but which has weathered well and now holds an assured place in London architecture'.[67] Mr David Piper wrote of 'the great Gothic phantasmagoria ... high as a cliff crowned with pinnacled castle in a Grimm's fairy-story, drawing up with complete confidence into its sky-assaulting rage of turrets the whole shabby, unresolved hotch-potch of the station area ... Its value to the London skyline is inestimable, and even more so as the rigour of concrete and glass envelopes more and more of London'.[68] The most generally acceptable judgment of the 1960s was that of Professor Nikolaus Pevsner:

'The building by Sir George Gilbert Scott is, side by side with the Foreign

Office (equally threatened), his best secular building. The train-shed by Barlow has lost nothing of its elegance and sweep through the one hundred years since it was designed. From the point of view of architecture and engineering neither can be spared.'[69]

There are still dissentients from such views. Mr Ian Nairn, for example, primly dismisses the hotel as 'incredibly clever in composition and incredibly heartless'.[70] Mr Furneaux Jordan, while admiring Barlow's roof without qualification, does not like the hotel and reiterates the criticism, long heard, that the building as a whole is the sum of two disparate parts. Train-shed and hotel together, he says, 'are perfect expression of that tragic schizophrenia that is Victorianism'. If, patronizingly, he concedes that 'Scott, in his vulgar way, pulled it off at St Pancras', it was by dint of ignoring 'that lovely iron roof'.[71] But are not Mr Jordan's generalizations too sweeping? One ends by wondering how carefully he has looked at the building himself. How can he say that Scott's Gothic detail 'was as elaborate on the back of the hotel as on the front'?[72] That statement is plainly untrue, as anyone can see who will take the trouble to go and look. Scott went to great pains, as we have seen, to insulate the hotel, in the interest of its guests, from the smoke and noise of the station. The simple treatment of its north face (easily visible now that the glass in the screen has been removed) was surely entirely appropriate: functionally, aesthetically, and as a proper observance of the economy that was constantly enjoined on him while the building was being erected.

In October 1967 Sir John Summerson accorded the building a characteristic 'cool appraisal', lauding Barlow, chiding Scott for his extravagance, for his departure from 'the reticent economy of some of his earlier works', while admitting that 'it is impossible not to admire Scott's enormous dexterity':

> 'This is not copy-book stuff; Scott really had Gothic in his head. Motifs of the best and purest kind sprang to his aid at every juncture. He was never at a loss for a profile or the ornament for a spandrel. No man now living could put on a performance like this.'

'Should St Pancras station and hotel together be preserved as a national monument?' asked Sir John in conclusion, giving the answer: 'If they can be rendered useful I do not see why not.'[73]

The genius presiding over the history of St Pancras station is Hardy's Spirit Ironic, and the Spirit is as active now as ever. Listen to the tone of this distinguished historian of our time, one whose opinion commands everybody's respect: tentative and tepid, totally without enthusiasm, coming in the end to this cautious conclusion, accurately couched in a

150

double negative. And contrast the certainty, the positive faith; the self-confidence, backed by a full knowledge of the grave penalties of failure; the largeness of scale that the building exemplifies, coupled with the consistent excellence of its craftsmanship. It is a perfect comment, none the less revealing for its silence, on the difference between the mid-Victorian world and our own.

[1] *Quarterly Review* 132 (1872), 301-3.

[2] *Recollections of Thomas Graham Jackson* (Oxford, 1950), 153. The article was, in fact, written by J T Emmett and reprinted in his *Six Essays* (1891; reprinted New York, 1972). His other work is on municipal reform, on leasehold, and on religious art and education. He revealed his identity as author of the essay in 1884.

[3] *Personal and Professional Recollections*, 262.

[4] cf. His remarks on pp. 268-9, 271.

[5] *Architect* 8 (1872), 227-8.

[6] *Edinburgh Review* 141 (1875), 396-404. This was in reply to a further article, plainly from the same hand, in *Quarterly Review* 137 (1874), 354-88.

[7] Like other critics who put forward such arguments, Fergusson shows no sign that he was acquainted with Barlow's detailed statement of the functional reasons for the adoption of the design: cf. pp. 35-9.

[8] J Fergusson, *History of the Modern Styles of Architecture* (2nd ed., 1873), 552-4.

[9] *Walks in London* (6th ed., 1894), i. 122. The building is not mentioned at all in the 5th edition of 1883.

[10] *Architect* 7 (1872), 2.

[11] N Pevsner, *The Buildings of England: the Cities of London and Westminster* (2nd ed., 1962), 341.

[12] *The Times*, March 28, 1878, 9.

[13] H Fry, *London in 1887* (1887), 243.

[14] Quoted in N Pevsner, *London except the Cities of London and Westminster* (1952), 368.

[15] The illustration is not sharp enough to be satisfactorily reproduced here.

[16] *English Illustrated Magazine* 10 (1892-93), 659.

[17] *Builder*, 27 February 1875, 191.

[18] *Ibid.*, 20 November 1875, 1,043.

[19] Great Eastern Railway half-yearly report, July 29, 1884: RAIL 227 / 145. (Robert Thorne), *Liverpool Street Station* (1978), 34-41.

[20] *Building News*, 2 June 1876, 557.

[21] C F D Marshall, *History of the Southern Railway* (1963 ed.), 345.

[22] G Dow, *Great Central* (1959-65), iii. 5.

[23] *Ibid.*, ii. 283.

[24] *Ibid.*, iii. 5.

[25] *Builder*, 10 April 1880, 439.

[26] *Builder*, 9 October 1875, 913; cf. also 19 June 1875, 545.

[27] It was designed by Charles Trubshaw, the Company's architect. For Sir Charles Reilly's devastating criticism of this huge and shapeless pile see his *Manchester Streets and their Buildings* (Liverpool, 1924), 57-60, and *Some Architectural Problems of To-day* (Liverpool, 1924), 74.

[28] Professor Meeks twice mistakenly states that the Midland Railway built the St Enoch station: *The Railway Station*, 86, 97.

[29] These stations are illustrated in Meeks, Figs. 113, 148, 151.

[30] *Ibid.*, 49.

[31] W J Lane, *Commodore Vanderbilt* (New York, 1942), 282.

[32] Meeks, 86-87, 100-01.

[33] *Ibid.*, 87, 101-02.

[34] *Ibid.*, 88, Fig. 102.

[35] *Ibid.*, 103-04, Figs. 104, 126. Professor Meeks also supplies a list of single roof spans exceeding 250 feet (p.115) and a table of large train-sheds built between 1845 and 1934 (pp.169-74).

[36] *Building News*, 20 March 1896, 419; John Physick and Michael Darby, *'Marble Halls'. Drawings and Models for Victorian Secular Buildings* (1973), 163.

[37] Quoted in Meeks, 96. Mr Briggs appears to have changed his mind subsequently. Over thirty years later he wrote of St Pancras that it 'is often bracketed with the Albert Memorial as his worst large design': *Architecture* (1947), 180.

[38] *The Gothic Revival* (1950 ed.), 9. Though Sir Kenneth subsequently modified many of the opinions he originally expressed, when he came to prepare the new edition of his book in 1949 he retracted none of his dislike of Scott, adding this footnote: 'He conquered the official and, so to say, the public-speaking world including a good many people who ought to have known better. But he never convinced the minority who really care' (*ibid.*, p.240).

[39] *Ibid.*, 258-9. Cf. p. 60 above.

[40] In his essay 'Our Big Railway Stations', reprinted in *Some Architectural Problems of To-day* (1924) he observes (p.35) that 'no architect of the first rank has been employed [by a railway company] since Hardwick at Euston'.

[41] My italics.

[42] *Journal of the Royal Institute of British Architects* 3rd ser. 46 (1939), 650-1.

[43] One does not know whether to attribute this gibe to Lord Stamp's ignorance or malevolence. The architect of Liverpool Cathedral was Scott's grandson.

[44] *Journal of the Royal Institute of British Architects* 3rd ser. 46 (1939), 658.

[45] *Railway Magazine* 89 (1943), 257; the Forshaw-Abercrombie *County of London Plan* of 1943 assumed that there would be six terminal stations north of the Thames with the facilities from St Pancras transferred to Euston.

[46] J M Richards, 'The Euston Murder', *Architectural Review*, 131 (April 1962), 234-8.

[47] Cf. pp. 124-5 above.

[48] *The Reshaping of British Railways* (1963), maps 1, 2, 9.

[49] *The Development of the Major Railway Trunk Routes* (1965), 40, 74.

[50] *Daily Telegraph*, August 26, 1966.

[51] *Guardian*, September 1, 1966, 8.

[52] *The Times*, September 3, 1966, 9.

[53] *The Times*, September 6, 1966, 9. Mr James Lees-Milne pointed out (September 10th, 9) that Sir Edward was 'the first person to have been a member of the Royal Fine Art Commission who publicly takes sides with the vandals'.

[54] *Ibid.*, September 15, 1966, 13.

[55] *Ibid.*, September 10, 1966, 9. Cf. Mr A. Trystan Edwards, *ibid.*, September 17, 1966, 9.

[56] *Ibid.*, September 9, 1966, 11.

[57] *The Times*, September 12, 1966, 11.

[58] *Ibid.*, September 13, 1966, 9.

[59] *Ibid.*, September 12, 1966, 11. One of the fruits of Mr de Maré's close study is the superb photograph of St Pancras against the setting sun reproduced in his *Photography and Architecture* (1961), 113.

[60] *Ibid.*, September 17, 1966, 16.

[61] *Daily Telegraph*, July 1, 1967, 19.

[62] *Ibid.*, September 20, 1967.

152

[63] Hansard, House of Lords, 5th series, vol. 278, cols. 1033-4.

[64] *Daily Telegraph,* November 3, 1967, 17.

[65] R Buckle, *The Adventures of a Ballet Critic* (1953), 105.

[66] J Betjeman, *First and Last Loves* (1952), 82-3.

[67] T S R Boase, *English Art, 1800-70* (1959), 252.

[68] D Piper, *Companion Guide to London* (1964), 310-11.

[69] *Guardian,* September 1, 1966, 8.

[70] I Nairn, *Nairn's London* (1966), 106.

[71] R F Jordan, *Victorian Architecture* (1966), 94-5.

[72] Ibid., 111.

[73] *Illustrated London News*, 7 October 1967, 17-19. See also John Summerson, *Victorian Architecture. Four Studies in Evaluation* (1970), 19-46.

CHAPTER VI

A Final Comment

ALMOST all the arguments that have raged round St Pancras station have been concerned with two things: function and style. How, in the end, are we to appraise them?

In functional terms as a station, St Pancras has worked well. There are weaknesses, as we have seen, in the design. But these arise in part from the nature of the site and from developments in railway operation inconceivable in the 1860s, when the building was planned. For all except a very few hours in the year it remains adequate for the traffic it handles. If it is to cease to be a station, that is because the management and operation of the British railway system have fundamentally changed.

The aesthetic qualities of the building are much more open to debate. Although it is now becoming fashionable to admire it, the weight of critical opinion, set out in the previous chapter, has on the whole been unfavourable. Emmett and Fergusson set the tone of it. No contemporary of equal power as a writer defended the building. And no one at all has tried seriously to expound just what Scott was attempting. The conventional view, from his time to ours, has been that he was merely supplying a decorative façade to the train-shed. It has been adjudged magnificent, flashy, tawdry, inappropriate, romantically exciting. But it ought to be considered historically, in the context of the 1860s. What, in his time, was Scott aiming at? How was he thinking?

Though pre-eminently a church architect, his secular work was considerable, and it would generally be agreed that it reaches its climax at St Pancras. When, in 1855-57, he wrote his *Remarks on Secular and Domestic Architecture, Present and Future,* he had two chief objects before him. First, he wished to show that the Gothic style, in his own hands and the hands of those who thought like him, was not a mere 'antiquarian movement', but 'pre-eminently free, comprehensive, and practical; ready to adapt itself to every change in the habits of society, to embrace every new material or system of construction, and to adopt implicitly and naturally, and with hearty good will, every invention or improvement, whether artistic, constructional, or directed to the increase of comfort and convenience'. And secondly, leading on from this, he contended that, though much had been done towards the improvement of churches, 'our civil architecture is as yet unrevolutionized'.[1]

At that time he was engaged on the first of his country houses, Pippbrook, Dorking. He had not yet erected any major public building for secular purposes. One can readily understand the eagerness with which he entered the competition for the new Foreign Office in 1856. The defeat he suffered there at the hands of Palmerston not only humiliated him personally: it deprived him of the opportunity of demonstrating the principles he had been working out, just at the time when they were at white heat in his mind. All that he had been thinking of, urging with so much energy, had now to be put to one side for another occasion. That occasion recurred only once. He failed to secure the commission for the Law Courts; his building for the University of Glasgow was *sui generis.* The chance he had so long desired came to him only at St Pancras. He was on fire to show 'that Gothic would admit of any degree of modernism'.[2] How could that be shown better than in a railway station and its hotel?

The decoration, as everyone has always recognized, is highly eclectic, with echoes of Winchester and Salisbury, of Amiens and Ypres and Venice. The building as a whole, in its grouping and mass, owes little to Italy and France, but something substantial to Flanders. That said, it is, most emphatically, of the nineteenth century, of the Railway Age. Scott saw no incongruity between his own work and Barlow's. The train-shed was a given fact before Scott's thinking began. Engineer and architect worked side by side on the station proper. Scott demonstrated there how perfectly his Gothic arcades and windows married with Barlow's curved iron girders, reaching up to their pointed apex: a form adopted, as we have seen, for no stylistic reason. What he aimed at throughout his task was a new synthesis between Gothic architecture and engineering. And, in a great measure, he found it.

The more one studies the great building as a whole, and in all its parts, the more one becomes convinced of the rightness of the solutions that Scott adopted to the problems that confronted him. Those who look at it with the eyes of the 1930s, trained in the Puritan spirit of the Modern Movement, will persist in seeing in it nothing but imitation, a moral falsehood. Can we not recognize that as a passing phase, a vagary of criticism; and return to Scott himself, to the tasks he had to perform, the pressures he was subject to, in the light of the history of his own mind? If so, we shall be able to see it, not indeed as a work without faults, but as a bold and noble achievement.

A FINAL COMMENT

There is no other building, in London or anywhere else, that embodies more precisely the achievement of mid-Victorian Britain. 'Precisely', because that achievement was above all an economic, an industrial and commercial one; and this is a commercial building. Its contemporaries – the Law Courts, provincial town halls like Waterhouse's at Manchester – are civic buildings: reflecting a long, distinguished tradition but not one that is in any sense special to the 1860s or even to the nineteenth century. St Pancras, on the other hand, is very much a monument of the economy and society of its own time. The train-shed reflects the skill, the boldness and certainty of the mid-Victorian engineer. He was working at a particular moment in the history of technology, when iron construction was at its zenith, on the very eve of the Age of Steel. A unique conjunction of difficulties faced him, to which his solution was precisely correct. Not many buildings so large and complicated can claim, in so great a degree, the finality of perfection.

If the train-shed is a demonstration of reason pursued to a logical conclusion, the hotel personifies romance, pursued almost as far. Just as Barlow drew on all his accumulated experience, and that of his contemporaries like Hawkshaw and Ordish, Scott concentrated thirty years' observation, and all his immense professional skill, into the task he had undertaken. He was an architect with a huge – an excessively huge – practice: yet he did not, as a modern *prima donna* architect might, neglect the building once the plans had been agreed on, leaving its execution to subordinates. Except on one relatively minor matter, towards the end, when one of his sons represented him, Scott dealt with the Midland Company himself. There were never any complaints of delay attributable to him or his staff. The disagreements that arose were of the kind most honourable to the architect, springing from his desire to see the building as well executed as possible, to prevent the adoption of those measures of economy in detail that are among the worst curses of an architect's life, often ruining the finish of his work in order to effect a saving that is ludicrously small. Scott had a very clear vision of what he wanted to do; and in the end, through his own patience and the steady tenacity of his clients, he did it, if not quite in accordance with his original intentions yet very near them. The complacency with which he speaks of the building himself is grotesque: but repellent though it may be, the root of it is not mere bombast, it is defiant and victorious pride.

His pride was well founded. The casing he designed to enclose the engineer's masterpiece is worthy of it: indeed, its ideal complement. In the train-shed the vermilion of the side walls helps to light up the roof. There have always been those who dislike the colour, no doubt because they found it too pungent.[3] But what other colour would have served so well? Dark red bricks or Staffordshire blue would have been sombre; yellow or white would

156

have turned a dirty, anonymous grey with the smoke of the years and offered no reflective contrast to the strong light pouring through the glass roof. This fiery effulgence is splendid: best of all as you enter the station on a morning train, the early light streaming in to pull out the powerful repeated curves of the girders, the whole vast hall aglow.

The treatment of the brickwork, too, is admirable. The Gothic doorways with their stone and marble dressings are strong enough to provide relief without creating fuss. The one purely decorative element, the brick-and-tile frieze at the cornice, reflects, horizontally and at right angles, the diapered metalwork of the principal ribs of the roof.

The interior of the hotel can be very imperfectly judged now. It has been turned over to uses for which it was never intended, most of the rooms divided up and shorn of their original fittings, the colour-schemes vanished beyond recall.[4] But it retains a noble amplitude, from the porch and reception hall along the curving corridor – still laid with its Minton tiles – to the grand staircase: grand indeed, and handsome in its details (though nearly every trace of Skidmore's gas fittings disappeared long since), soaring up four stories to its vaulted roof, irradiated through tall windows with the western light. Climb up to the top of the building, and this amplitude everywhere continues: in the scale of the servants' bedrooms on the fifth and sixth floors; in the huge timber-framed cavern of the west tower. Out on the roof among the chimney-stacks you get one of the great experiences of London. Near at hand is the avenue of chimneys, rich crimson brick rising from limestone bases washed white with a hundred years' rain; at the end of the avenue the clock tower. And what a clock too, with its splendid dial in blue, white, black, and gold – by immemorial custom still wound up on Tuesdays, and always kept two minutes fast, to speed on passengers arriving late.[5] Southward, St Paul's hemmed in now by the ignoble clobber of recent commercial building; to the north, the long line of Barlow's roof, pointing out to the heights of Hampstead, and down there to the left, screened closely in trees, old St Pancras church standing in the grave-yard that was so ruthlessly mauled by the railway.

In the street, as you wait for a westbound bus, the dark red mass of Scott's building towers over you, springing up from its vast sloping plinth: asymmetrical, yet perfectly balanced in its parts. But you catch the magic of the building best from a distance: from high up on the Pentonville Road – O'Connor's point of vantage in the 'eighties, still affording the same unforgettable view at sunset; from the north, beyond the goods station, in Purchese Street; or driving up from the West End through the dull waste land beyond Russell Square, catching your first glimpse of the high pinnacled western tower. It is a momentary sight, fleeting and improbable, lost at once behind the intervening blocks of flats, to be picked up again for another moment, and again lost; until the whole astonishing pile, in its full majesty, bursts on you as you turn out of Judd Street into the Euston Road.

For me – and, as I know, for many other people – St Pancras station is a building that exercises the force of life itself. To remove it would be to impoverish not merely a street but a whole quarter of London. If we truly care for what we have inherited from the past, if our love for the Victorian age is real and not just a fashionable craze, then we must find means to keep it.

Sir John Summerson agrees that the station and hotel should be preserved 'if they can be rendered useful'. It is there indeed that the heart of the problem lies. The demands of the 1860s have changed entirely by the 1960s. A railway exists to handle traffic, or it is nothing. If it can be demonstrated that the traffic of the old Midland Railway can be handled more efficiently and cheaply elsewhere, then St Pancras must cease to be a station. But it cannot remain empty, a vast, useless museum exhibit. Can the hotel return to its original purpose? Given capital, imagination, and technical skill, informed by a kindling enthusiasm, it might well be possible. If the train-shed must cease to house trains, let it look back to the rock whence it was hewn. The Crystal Palace is gone. Its poor relation the Alexandra Palace is moribund. Why should not Barlow's masterpiece supply some of the facilities they afforded, an epitome and an enduring memorial of the great age that conceived it?

[1] *Remarks on Secular and Domestic Architecture* (1857), viii, 13.

[2] *Personal and Professional Recollections*, 376.

[3] *Architect* (6 February 1869), 77.

[4] Here Jack Simmons was mistaken. Some of the original colour schemes have survived beneath later over-painting, including dazzling schemes executed by Frederick Sang.

[5] Alas! The St Pancras clocks have deteriorated while these pages were passing through the press. This clock has been stopped for months, and the big one inside the building against the south screen is now permanently disused and divested of its hands, in favour of insignificant electric clocks, imperfectly visible from many parts of the station.

CHAPTER VII

St Pancras Revived
by Robert Thorne

W hen the first edition of this book was published in 1968 the future of St Pancras station was still in doubt. True, it has been listed the year before and its supporters had been ex tremely effective in making the case for keeping it, but the plans by British Railways to divert its trains to Euston, King's Cross and Moorgate were still being actively considered. Jack Simmons set out to pro vide a rounded history of the station from its inception till the crisis in its history in the 1960s, and he gave that narrative an unmistakably polemical thrust. It is clear why he decided to write the book, and we are left in no doubt about his admiration for the station and for those who built it. As John Betjeman said, he produced a 'readable, learned and inspiring book'[1]. Although it was published after the first wave of controversy generated by the British Railways proposals was over, it helped confirm St Pancras as a building of international importance.

While Simmons was completing his book in early 1968 the debate about the station continued. It was a sign of the attention it attracted, and of the changing attitude to Victorian buildings generally, that the Duke of Edin burgh agreed to chair a meeting at Buckingham Palace about its future. What is interesting about that gathering, which Jack Simmons attended, is that the discussion assumed that the station and hotel would be kept even if not in railway use: the idea of demolition, which seemed a real threat only two years previously, was no longer actively countenanced. If bereft of trains, the best alternative uses for Barlow's shed appeared to be either as an indoor sports centre – it could hold fifteen tennis courts – or as a museum of industrial archaeology. Meanwhile the hotel could be reopened in its original use. Roderick Gradidge, an architect and member of the Victorian Society, had shown how that could be done and his ideas had been taken up by the hotelier Maxwell Joseph. He described to the Buckingham Palace meeting a blissfully profitable future for the whole complex: "if British Rail ways sell the site for £1 million, and if modernising the hotel cost another

£1 million, and making the exhibition centre in the train shed a further £1 million, making £3 million in all, the hotel would earn 7 or 8 per cent on the whole £3 million capital".[2]

But ultimately these deliberations, and the involvement of royalty, were a waste of time. Just before Christmas 1968, when it was hoped the announcement would pass unnoticed, British Railways let it be known that train services to St Pancras had been reprieved: it was uneconomic to direct them elsewhere.[3] So the episode which began two years previously, and which led Jack Simmons to write this book, simply fizzled out.

There was however a curious tailpiece to the dispute of 1966-68 about the station's merits, which brought the old warring parties to life again. It concerned the booking hall which, after its partial refurbishment in 1957, was still recognisably the room which Scott had designed, with its polychromatic brickwork and sculptured corbels incorporating figures of busy railwaymen. Above all, the original ticket office had survived, a linenfold panelled structure which sat against the east wall of the booking-hall, looking like a leftover from a Tudor manor house. The location of this ticket office, facing the taxi road on the west side of the station, reflected the way that most passengers originally arrived at St Pancras; but once the majority of people began to come by subways from the underground directly to the concourse, its position conflicted with the way the station was used. And also, in the eyes of British Railways, its historical design was at odds with the contemporary idiom of a modernised railway operation.

Because the booking hall seemed such an anomaly, in 1978 British Railways decided to redesign the ticket office as a travel centre in a wholly modern, rectangular style. But since the station was now listed there was a formal procedure to be followed to gain permission for such an alteration. Objectors, led by the Victorian Society and including Jack Simmons, argued that the ticket office was an integral part of Scott's masterpiece and that, adapted and repositioned against the west wall of the booking hall, it could continue to give admirable service. This was essentially a rerun in miniature of the earlier arguments between railway operators and architectural conservationists, enlivened by a sense of indignation that British Railways apparently still did not appreciate the importance of the station in all its aspects. The case went to Public Inquiry and ultimately in 1980 the Secretary of State for the Environment, as final arbiter, decided in the Victorian Society's favour. As they had suggested, the ticket office was relocated where it could be better seen by passengers, and no doubt today most people think that is where it has always stood.[4]

This booking hall dispute touched on the larger question of the future of St Pancras. Part of the argument for altering the station was to do with the number of passengers it was handling, but at the time of the Public Inquiry that number was static and plans were being made that would eventually reduce it. Since 1960, the suburban services to Luton and Bedford had used diesel multiple units, but in 1976 it was decided to electrify the line as far as Bedford using a 25Kv ac system. Under the dreadful nickname of the BedPan service, electric suburban trains started running into St Pancras in 1983: the same service was also connected to Moorgate in the City of London using the link from the Midland line that had first opened in 1868.[5] No sooner had it been introduced than the Greater London Council asked about the possibility of reopening the connection between Farringdon, on the branch to Moorgate, and Blackfriars. This link, one of the very few cross-London railway connections, had been used mainly by freight trains. What the GLC recognised was that it offered the chance for passenger journeys from north to south of the Thames without changing and, more to the point, it could deliver commuters closer to where they needed to be. The publicity for this proposal suggested the allure of journeys from Bedford to Brighton or Luton to Sutton, but what really mattered was that commuters from either direction could stay on their train to Farringdon or Blackfriars, rather than have to change to the underground. One obvious by-product of this proposal was that suburban trains from the north, most of which still terminated at St Pancras, would instead be diverted into the route across London; the station would thus be deprived of some of its staple traffic.

The extraordinary thing about the Thameslink service, as it was named, was how quickly it was introduced; perhaps because it made such obvious good sense, but also because it used entirely existing lines. The main works involved – relaying the track between Farringdon and Blackfriars, plus new signalling – cost only about £4 million: the main expenditure was on new trains equipped for both third rail electric traction on the lines south of Farringdon and overhead traction on the BedPan route. Government approval of the project was given in 1985 and the first trains started running three years later, one of the most creative legacies of the GLC which by then had been abolished. From that time very few suburban trains have used St. Pancras: instead they dive into a tunnel at Kentish Town which takes them under the west side of the station and under the hotel before emerging at the separate Thameslink station on Pentonville Road.[6]

Meanwhile the hotel was still eking out an existence as railway offices, with some staff bedrooms in the garrets, but even that came to an end in 1985 when its lack of fire escapes let to its being declared unsafe to occupy. Stripped of all its furnishings it became totally redundant and open to the risks that any empty building faces. In 1988 fire damaged part of its west wing.

Once it had lost its suburban traffic, and with the hotel closed and deserted,

St Pancras Station was manifestly too large for the modest functions it then served – essentially two main line trains an hour, one to Nottingham and one to Sheffield. It could still be appreciated almost exactly as Barlow and Scott had designed it, and it appeared to be under no immediate threat, but much of the life had gone out of its existence. But that was about to change more dramatically than anyone could have envisaged, for reasons only indirectly to do with its original functions.

*   *   *   *

The most important of these changes can only be understood by looking at St Pancras in its wider context, especially its relationship to its old rival King's Cross. At the same time as the Great Northern Railway built King's Cross Station it established an extensive goods yard just to the north, beyond the Regent's Canal. It was a carefully thought out project, designed to handle agricultural produce, fish, regular goods and coal: for a time the Midland Railway shared its facilities. The Great Northern could justly claim to have helped transform the supply of foodstuffs and other commodities to London, and the yard was one of the most important of its kind.[7] But after the Second World War that system of supply slid into decline as road transport became pre-eminent. It was the same change of fortune which signalled the fate of the Midland's Somers Town Goods Depot, and the decision in 1975 to redevelop that site as the new British Library.

As a redevelopment site the King's Cross Goods Yard seemed a tempting prize: an area of at least 60 acres (or more, if the gasworks to the south of the canal were included) close to a major transport interchange. Under pressure from a Conservative Government, British Railways felt obliged to maximise the return from its surplus properties, and a large site so close to the centre of London was an obvious candidate for disposal. An example of what might be achieved was provided by the Broadgate development, just to the north of the City of London. Work there began in 1985, on land previously occupied by Broad Street Station and its adjoining goods yard, and it helped enable Liverpool Street Station to be transformed. As many property experts had predicted, in 1987 it became clear that the King's Cross Goods Yard was the next big railway site to be offered for redevelopment.

But that was only the beginning, and it was the next episode involving this development which ultimately was most significant for St Pancras. 1987 was also the year when work began on the Channel Tunnel, and it was planned that initially trains from Europe would arrive at Waterloo travelling over existing tracks from the Channel. There were two disadvantages to that arrangement: it was difficult to engineer a purpose-built line to

Waterloo, to enable high speed Eurostar trains to travel as fast in England as they would do on the continent, and it was impossible for trains once they had reached Waterloo to continue onwards to the Midlands and North of England. Members of Parliament from northern constituencies were insistent that this new railway should benefit the whole of the country, not just London and the South-East. King's Cross seemed the ideal place to connect Eurostar trains with routes to the north, with the added benefit that the redevelopment of the goods yard could pay for the new international station which ultimately would replace Waterloo. So although early in 1987 it had been denied before a House of Lords Committee that King's Cross could ever be a station for Channel Tunnel trains, by October that year the developers bidding for the goods yard site were told to include that facility in their proposals.[8] The intention was to repeat at King's Cross the formula which seemed to be working so well at Broadgate and Liverpool Street.

The success of the King's Cross project depended on the selection of a developer with a suitable scheme, and the negotiation of the necessary consents: an Act of Parliament for the station and railway approaches, not unlike the Acts which had sanctioned the building of St Pancras and King's Cross in the first place, and planning permission for the redevelopment of the goods yard. The London Regeneration Consortium was chosen in June 1988, a company which included the developers involved at Broadgate, and before the end of the year the King's Cross Railways Bill had been laid before Parliament. The proposal which the consortium put forward, designed by Foster Associates, envisaged an international station built diagonally beneath King's Cross station, served by a new concourse between King's Cross and St. Pancras on the site of the Great Northern Hotel. Trains would reach the new station in tunnel from the south, and could proceed onwards to connect with the main lines to the Midlands and the north. There were to be eight platforms, because the station would be used by south-east commuter trains and Thameslink trains as well as international trains: this was crucial because local trains could attract public funding, whereas international services were prohibited from receiving subsidy. The enabling development, stretching over 134 acres from the northern end of the King's Cross Goods Yard to the triangle between the main stations, was to consist chiefly of commercial office buildings arranged around a roughly oval open space north and south of the Regent's Canal. Isolated in the midst of that space were one or two surviving goods yard buildings, reminders of its more workaday past. St Pancras was left untouched, but some of its approach tracks were to be decked over to form the western edge of the development.

Seen in the Foster drawings, or the splendid models that were produced, the London Regeneration Consortium scheme seemed bold yet plausible, but it was far more complex than anything like it that had been previously been built. It relied upon immensely onerous and costly engineering for the construction of the low level station beneath King's Cross and the new approach tunnels. At the same time the partial funding of those works from the new development presupposed a level of profit to be gained for the new commercial offices. One study put the cost of the low level station at £830 million, but the profit from the sale of the development area at only £280 million.[9] The collapse in office demand in the early 1990s called into question how far that cross-financing of the new station could be relied on, and at the same time the government grew nervous about how the funding gap might be filled. Although the King's Cross Railways Bill went through most of its parliamentary stages, its progress began to falter in 1992. When the Chancellor, Norman Lamont, failed to announce sufficient funding for the project in his budget statement in November that year it was clear that the scheme had hit an impasse.

This is where St Pancras came back into the picture. In 1990 the engineers Ove Arup Partnership had promoted the idea of bringing Channel Tunnel trains to King's Cross via East London, with a stop at Stratford, rather than through the southern suburbs as previously proposed. This found favour with a government anxious to regenerate Docklands and East London, and was adopted as the route in October 1991.[10] The realignment of the route encouraged many people, especially engineers not committed to the King's Cross low level scheme, to look afresh at where the international station would be sited. One firm, Alan Baxter & Associates, suggested that it should be built as a separate station with its own identity in the heart of the goods yard, away from the congestion of facilities at King's Cross.[11] Others turned their attention to St Pancras, whose half empty platforms seemed to be crying out for a new role. If the new line was coming from the east rather than the south it could approach along the route of the North London Line, either above or below ground, before sweeping into St Pancras across the goods yard. It seemed obvious that adapting St Pancras would be cheaper than building a new station in tunnel beneath King's Cross, and it would decisively remove St Pancras from the danger list.

When he designed St Pancras, W H Barlow made the case for a single arch trainshed on the grounds that it would provide flexibility for changes in railway operation, but he never dreamed of a change as dramatic as the Channel Tunnel Rail Link. He thought that the platform layout might be altered, but he never envisaged having to accommodate 18-coach Eurostar trains which would reach far beyond the length of the trainshed and demand a complete reorganisation of the approach tracks to the station. He gave careful thought to how arriving and departing passengers and goods would be handled – a system which served the station extremely well – yet it did not occur to him to anticipate a time when trains would be three times the length of the ones he knew and passengers would have to be herded through customs inspection. In other words, although it was easy to assume that a much underused station would make an ideal Channel Tunnel terminus, the works involved to make that a reality were just as onerous as those which had confronted Barlow and his colleagues.

It became generally known late in 1992 that the St Pancras proposal was being lobbied for by some within British Railways, despite the fact that the King's Cross Bill was still before Parliament.[12] Development of the proposal took place furtively behind closed doors. More was learnt about it a few months later when the *Observer* revealed that the architect involved was Nick Derbyshire, fresh from his triumphantly successful work at Liverpool Street.[13] Work continued throughout 1993, always under the pretence that King's Cross was still the front runner and that St Pancras was a notional alternative. But it came as no surprise when John MacGregor, Secretary of State for Transport, announced in January 1994 that the Government had withdrawn the King's Cross Bill and that St Pancras was now to be the international terminus.[14] As with the previous turnaround in 1968 there was almost no comment on the colossal waste of money and effort represented by the rejection of the King's Cross scheme.

The ideas that were emerging for St Pancras were still linked to the future of the King's Cross Goods Yard because they depended on a complex series of tunnels and viaducts on the northern part of the site to join St Pancras to the new international route and other lines. Having come in tunnel from Stratford, the Channel Tunnel Rail Link was to emerge to the east of the goods yard before crossing the Regent's Canal and entering the station. Other lines would join the CTRL to the North London Line and the East Coast line from King's Cross. Meanwhile Thameslink, which was to retain its existing route beneath St Pancras, was to acquire a tunnelled connection to the King's Cross line so that commuter trains from places such as Cambridge and Peterborough could run through London, just as trains from Bedford and Luton had been doing since 1988. In the now discarded King's Cross proposal it had been intended that Thameslink would share the new low level station, but now it was to be given its own below ground station on the west side of St Pancras.

In the terminus itself, the original platform length and layout had been restricted by the gasworks to the north, in particular the gasholders erected at the same time as the station. Those gasholders, heightened in the 1880s and added to in number, were about to be decommissioned thus removing one fundamental impediment to the extension of St Pancras; but three which stood in the way of that extension had been listed, and so would have to be dismantled for re-erection elsewhere *(plate XII)*. There was also a locomotive watering-point just beyond the end of the platform, listed because of its affinity to the station: that too would have to be moved. If those structures could be dealt with, and the adjoining roads realigned, the problem of having to lengthen the station by about 250 metres (273 yards) began to look resolvable; but the extension, like the original station, would still have to be on a viaduct about 4.8 metres (16 ft) above street level.

It was not just a question of length: width was also a problem. The existing station had seven platforms, but now it was expected to house thirteen – six for international trains, three for commuter trains that would use the same route from Kent, and four for Midland line trains. They couldn't all be fitted into Barlow's shed, but if the station was extended sideways more of the neighbouring buildings (some of them listed) would have to be demolished, removing yet another part of the station's original context. It felt increasingly like squeezing a quart into a pint pot.

Some of the problems in converting St Pancras had already been thought about in the design of Waterloo International, which was completed in 1993. In particular Waterloo was also a station on a viaduct above the street, and the solution there was to deal with both arriving and departing passengers in the undercroft beneath the platforms using a segregated circulation system like an airport. Nick Derbyshire was uncomfortable about applying the same formula to St Pancras, partly because he wanted to keep as much as possible of Barlow's undercroft with its rhythm of iron columns and beams, but even more because he thought passengers should enjoy the trainshed rather than be trapped below platform level. He therefore proposed redeveloping a semi-derelict area on the west (Midland Road) side of the station as the international departure area, from which passengers would go by escalator and bridge to their trains, with views down the trainshed from the gable end.[15] Arriving passengers, who have less reason to linger, would be taken down to a new undercroft beneath the station extension and so out into the street just beyond the original building. In his plan some of the Midland line trains would come into the trainshed alongside the Channel Tunnel trains, but the commuter trains would stop short of the trainshed on the east side: they would disgorge their passengers, mainly to the underground, via a concourse which incorporated the remarkable German Gymnasium, another survivor from the time when St Pancras was first built.

Having sorted out the circulation of the different types of passenger, Derbyshire had to confront the other main dilemma in designing the extension – how to add to Barlow's shed without detracting from its integrity *(plate XI)*. There were some who argued that the only logical thing to do was to

replicate the arched form of the existing structure, yet that was functionally difficult because the new addition had to be wider than the original station; and anyway, there has always been a presumption amongst those
dealing with old buildings that new work should be clearly distinguishable
from the old. Others said that the extension should have simple platform
canopies, so low that they would never compete with Barlow's shed. That
seemed too modest – and perhaps draughty – for such a major facility. With
the help of the engineer Tony Hunt (who had worked on Waterloo International) Derbyshire developed the idea of a new roof as a series of shallow arches suspended from masts which aligned with the walls of the original trainshed, the whole covering having a slight curve but one which would
not compete with Barlow's arch. This made good sense except in one respect: the three commuter platforms on the east side had to be given a separate roof, a smaller version of the main one, which inevitably looked like an
afterthought. Maybe it was right that the different uses of the new station should be expressed separately, but the result was a loss of clarity
compared with the layout for which St Pancras was famous.

But whatever dissensions there might be from Nick Derbyshire's proposals they were fundamental in helping address the transformation that
St Pancras was to undergo. More to the point, they formed the basis of the
so-called reference case attached to the Bill that was put before Parliament
to build the Channel Tunnel Rail Link. The original Bill to sanction the
building of St Pancras in 1863 had only a map showing the extent of the
proposed site, within what were known as the limits of deviation, but now far
more detail was called for especially on the environmental consequences of the
works. The Bill presented in 1994 was designated a Hybrid Bill because
the project, though developed within the public sector, was to be carried
forward by a private sector developer. Indeed it was seen as a model project
of this kind for infrastructure works and, to the fury of those who had fought
for St Pancras over the years, the Bill included provision to disapply the
normal listed building controls and substitute specially drafted minimum
requirements. So relief that St Pancras had been given a substantial new
role, with a scheme that was momentous but unobjectionable, was qualified by
anxiety that the detailed quality of the original building might be lost.[16]

The most conspicuous difference between the original Bill and its 1994
successor was that in the 1860s there was no doubt that it would be the
Midland Railway which, once empowered, would build the London extension and station; whereas in the 1990s it was always known that Union
Railways, the part of British Railways which promoted the new Bill, would
select a developer to design, build and operate the new Channel Tunnel
route. Thus two parallel processes took place: the ponderous passage of the

enabling legislation through Parliament and the equally protracted business of selecting the developer. By March 1995, when the House of Commons Select Committee was hearing evidence on the Bill, bids were received from four development consortia: by July that number had been reduced to two. In February 1996 the bidding process ended with the announcement that London and Continental Railways Ltd. would be the so-called 'nominated undertaker' for the works in the Bill; but the Bill itself was not finally passed until nine months later.[17]

The route from the Channel Tunnel to St Pancras is not that far – 108km (67 miles) – but such is the difficulty and cost of constructing a new high speed railway through a densely inhabited corner of England that London and Continental is inevitably a more complex company than the Midland Railway ever was; a consortium of engineering, transport and financial firms brought together to provide the combined expertise required. Where St Pancras is concerned it is the engineering and construction members that matter most – the American project managers Bechtel, the French rail consultants Systra, the engineers Halcrow, and perhaps above all Arups, who having persuaded the Government to adopt an eastern approach route to London then helped show in detail how it could be built. What was equally important was that the architects Foster and Partners were brought in to act as masterplanners for the station design; a return to a part of London familiar to them from their earlier ill-fated King's Cross project.

At St Pancras what London and Continental have done is to reshape the station design by Nick Derbyshire that was put before Parliament, at first through the masterplan provided by Fosters and subsequently through detailed design by architects from within the consortium led by Alastair Lansley (plates XIII-XIV). The shape of the station design has remained fundamentally the same – it could hardly be otherwise given the constraints of the site and the length of the platforms needed for international trains – but the relationship between the Barlow trainshed and the new construction has been significantly altered. Instead of the bridge across the trainshed which Derbyshire proposed as the way to get departing passengers to their trains, they now will come up to the platforms from below. So they will see more of the structure of the undercroft than originally planned, but may have less time to savour Barlow's roof. The undercroft, which until now has been a Stygian world known only to railwaymen and business tenants, will be brought into the life of the station as the main circulation space for international travellers. This is made possible because the roof of the undercroft is to be restructured by laying a reinforced concrete raft on top of Barlow's wrought iron beams and arches, taking the load from the beams and enabling breaks in the structural grid to be made. Some of these breaks will be for the travelators which will take people up to their trains, but the more daring change is to be the insertions of four long lightwells in the roof of the undercroft on the west side. Thanks to these lightwells departing passengers will be able to see a cross-section of the station while they wait below. Those arriving from abroad will also go down into the undercroft as their route out of the station.

Using the undercroft makes sense because in fact it is at street level and so can easily be opened up to the flanking streets, as well as to the wide transverse concourse that will mark the transition from the original station to the new extension. The station will be far less of a barrier across the area than it has been so far. The transverse concourse will be the main way that people enter the station from the street and the underground; not just travellers going abroad but commuters, passengers for the Midland main line, and people using Thameslink. Above them will be the tracks and platforms going into the Barlow trainshed, and from the concourse will be escalators to the shorter domestic platforms. Derbyshire wanted to have at least one Midland line platform beneath the Barlow roof but now those trains, which being diesel – powered are too filthy for the restored station, are all to be banished to the west side of the new extension. The commuter trains from Kent will be on the east side. Across the station as a whole there will be one less platform in the original trainshed but a total of thirteen platforms in all.

As for the roof of the new extension, this has got simpler (*ill. 50*). In place of Derbyshire's shallow suspended arches it is now a flat, north-lit roof across all the platforms, carried on four lines of columns, two down the perimeter and two down the centre. As a concept this may not appear all that different to a previous generation of flat-roofed trainsheds, such as Glasgow Central or the early twentieth century roof at Waterloo, but it is far superior in clarity; and in sheer scale there is nothing quite like it – 220 metres (721ft) long, carried 20 metres (65ft) above street level. In an age when the prevailing urge (at least in Britain) is to hide stations beneath office blocks it has the immense benefit of being naturally lit, both from the sides and above. The details of the top glazing are perhaps not as overtly sculptural as was first intended, but for most people that may not matter: what is important is that it will feel like a proper station, with nothing timid or apologetic about it.[18]

When St Pancras was first built it was in the hands of three contractors – Waring Bros. for the main station works, the Butterley Company for the roof and Jackson & Shaw for the hotel – and the overall cost was £1million. Now there are at least eight main contractors involved, and the contract work for the extension and refurbishment of the station, without the hotel, is £311 million.

* * * *

As Jack Simmons made clear, when St Pancras was first built the construction of the station progressed ahead of work on the hotel: indeed the
completed Midland Grand did not finally open until eight years after the
station. Yet the two parts were always regarded as being inseparably linked.
Likewise in the recent history of the building, in parallel with the development of the new station there has been another saga unfolding, one which
concerns the quest to bring the hotel back into use with the aim of its
reopening at the same time as Eurostar trains first arrive at the station. As
in the original construction project the two sides of the story constantly connect and overlap, but the scheme to rejuvenate the Midland Grand (which
in early 2003 was less advanced than the station works) has many aspects
worth attention on their own.

Ever since Maxwell Joseph's confident predictions for the future of the
building in 1968 the idea of its being brought back into use, most obviously
as a hotel, had never completely died; but as long as the area around St
Pancras and King's Cross was gripped by indecision and blight no-one came
forward to take up the cause. However that began to change in the late
1980s, at the time when the redevelopment of the King's Cross Goods Yard
was first contemplated. One of the consortia which bid for the goods yard
project was headed by the developers Speyhawk and Sir Robert McAlpine
& Sons, using as their architects York, Rosenberg and Mardell. The same
team put together a proposal for the Midland Grand which was submitted
for planning permission in August 1987, just as the debate about the whole
area was gathering momentum.

As this Speyhawk proposal showed, it was never going to be easy to
bring the hotel to life again[19]. Despite its original success in many ways it
was an awkward building, which could only be made to work with an army
of hotel servants. This was not just a matter of its lack of bathrooms and
lavatories, its most evident defect. Although it was brilliantly integrated
with the station, its entrances were poorly located and its overall shape
meant that wherever guests entered they inevitably had a long walk to their
rooms. Above all, its vertical layout, reflected in every detail down to
furnishings and floor coverings, embodied a mid-Victorian sense of hierarchy;
a far cry from the late twentieth century ideal of uniform rooms at every level.

The Speyhawk approach to these problems was to separate the building
into different functions. At its heart it would again be a hotel, with 127
bedrooms, but the top two floors would be siphoned off as apartments and
the wing which curves towards the Euston Road would become a hotel club,

170

48. *Damaged gable end at the hotel, 1990.*

49. *Eroded brickwork, 1990.*

complete with a Turkish bath in the old basement kitchen. This range of functions would mean that it attracted more than just hotel guests. But even more important, the proposal included the conversion of the station undercroft as a retail area, designated a speciality shopping centre in the terminology of the time. This was to have its own atrium in the area north of the taxi road. What is obvious, though not made explicit in the way the project was described, is that this retail element was crucial to helping finance the restoration of the hotel. Simply to restore and reopen the hotel on its own wasn't a viable proposition.

This scheme was granted planning permission in 1989 but like other projects in the area, notably the goods yard development, it faded from view in the property recession of the early 1990s; and once the undercroft had been reserved for railway use as part of the CTRL scheme for St Pancras it lost the retail component on which it depended. That left the building as an encumbrance to British Railways, at a time when rail privatisation was in the air and a huge historic building without a use was the last thing a future railway operator wanted. Yet out of the apparently despondent situation following the demise of the Speyhawk proposal came a welcome bonus for the future of the building.

It was obvious by 1990 that the hotel, having been left empty and largely uncared for, was deteriorating if not unsafe. An architectural firm, the Conservation Practice, were asked to make a survey of safety, followed by a more detailed condition survey. What they found was alarming: eroded brick and stonework, slates slipped and broken, rusting ironwork and dry

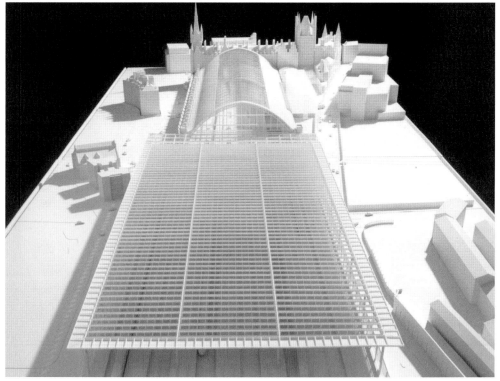

50. View of the model, showing the north lit roof over the extended platforms.

rot *(ills 48-49)*. None of this was the fault of Scott's original design, though if he'd known the conditions the building was to suffer he might have chosen some materials differently. The hotel simply had not been given the routine maintenance that every building needs, with the result that problems of every kind had taken hold. A short contract followed, to secure the most dangerous features and stop the worst of the weather getting in. Then in 1993-5 the whole of the exterior was repaired and restored at a cost of £9 million, an extraordinary investment by British Railways, which by the time the work had finished had ceased to exist as a nationalized body. But the timing was significant. The restoration began when the idea of St Pancras as the Channel Tunnel terminus was being actively canvassed, and it gave a clear indication that it was the favoured alternative. Symbolically it prepared the way for the Channel Tunnel project.

Perhaps the most important aspect of these restoration works was on the skyline: the reslating of the roof using some recycled slates but mostly new ones from Westmoreland, the repair of the dormers, new zinc for the finials and flat roofs, and the repair or remaking of the ironwork cresting. At the lower levels, damaged brickwork was repaired or replaced, and newly-carved Ketton or Ancaster stone was used where the original stonework was too far eroded. The structure was cleaned using sensitive, low pressure systems. And the statue of Britannia on the east wing was dismantled, restored and put back, to look down once again on the Midland's rival at King's Cross[20].

These were all external works, except in one important respect. When the condition survey of the building was done the chance was taken to investigate some of the interior decorative schemes; to remove darkened layers of dirt, varnish and overpainting to disclose original stencilling and other finishes. In particular the paintings of the eight virtues in the vault at the head of the grand staircase were examined, revealing that they were in a parlous state. Not only had they been overpainted and crudely repaired, but water in the plasterwork from leaking roofs had led the paintwork to blister and peel. This was a problem too urgent to wait for decisions about the full reuse of the building, so it was decided to clean and restore the vault and its paintings *(plate VII)*. One of the virtue panels, Humility, had been so damaged by water that a new copy on canvas had to be made and fixed to a renewed plasterwork base. The result of this restoration project was that at least the grand staircase could be enjoyed in something like its original state[21].

Once the scaffolding had come down on the freshly cleaned and restored exterior passers-by could be forgiven for thinking that the future of the hotel was secure, but in fact the debate about its future was only just beginning. Not long after the completion of the exterior restoration London and Continental Railways took control of the building as part of the agreement for the development of the Channel Tunnel Rail Link. Although it might be argued that the building was not really a part of the railway project, LCR felt that it was so conspicuously linked to the station that they had to take it in hand. In September 1996 they organised a competition to find a new use for the building, with no fixed preconception about what that use might be. After making a shortlist of eight in January 1998 they selected the Chambers Group, a consortium consisting of the Whitbread Hotel Company (backed by Marriott Hotels) and the Manhattan Loft Company, a firm well known for its imaginative ventures in creating flats in existing buildings.

Like everyone who has ever thought about the future of the building, the Chambers Group was naturally drawn to the idea of reopening it as a hotel. Although it had failed in that function some sixty years previously that seemed the logical choice, confirmed by how inappropriate it had felt when used by the railways as offices. But like the earlier Speyhawk proposal, the Chambers Group discovered that to have just a hotel use in the existing building would not be viable. The sheer expense of restoring Scott's principal interiors, and introducing new facilities, meant that the solution had to be something more than just a return to its original use. As with the Speyhawk scheme it was decided to have two floors of apartments in the topmost, dormered storeys, converting spaces which would not make good hotel bedrooms. But having subtracted those floors, plus the first floor for conference uses, there was insufficient space for the number of bedrooms needed to make the hotel work. So the Chambers Group proposed a new extension, to be built on the west side of the station in a derelict area due to be demolished as part of the railway project. With that extension, plus the rooms in the original building, they could achieve a 283 bedroom hotel; a size large enough not just to restore Scott's legacy, including the taxi road and the booking hall, but to fill it again with life and activity.

Other surviving terminus hotels, some of them discussed by Jack Simmons in Chapter V, have been dramatically refurbished in recent years – the Great Western at Paddington, the Hotel Great Central at Marylebone and the Great Eastern at Liverpool Street. They help give confidence that railway hotels still have a future, based on the glamour of their original function. If anywhere deserves a hotel it is St Pancras, now that it is to become an international terminus. But the Midland Grand is not quite like the other examples which have recently been transformed. First of all it is a building of much greater significance, which therefore deserves to be treated in a more exacting and conscientious way; and secondly, unlike the others, it long ago lost its original use. By early 2003 the proposals for it had been further developed but the design of the new extension was still in its infancy. The need for that extension, and how it will appear, looks destined to generate just as much excitement as Scott's first competition entry.

*   *   *   *

As this new edition of Jack Simmons' book goes to print the scene at the north end of the station is strikingly similar to the views of the original construction works published in the illustrated press of 1867-8 *(ill. 51)*. Most of the gasholders have gone, the frames of some of them stacked ready to be re-erected. Roads have been diverted from their familiar routes. The original viaduct that brought trains into the station has been half demolished, to be replaced by the new concrete substructure of the station extension. In the far distance the routes for international trains and Thameslink across the King's Cross Goods Yard are beginning to take shape. And as if that were not enough, in front of St Pancras a huge excavation of the forecourt verifies that at last the long-promised improvements to the underground station are in progress. All in all it is a positively Victorian spectacle of energy and activity.[22]

51. *Work in progress on the International Terminus, spring 2003, looking north from the top of Barlow's trainshed.*

When all the works have been completed, and the station and hotel reopened in their new role, no doubt journalists will cling to this analogy with a previous railway age. The transformation will be described as a decisive and heroic project that Barlow and Scott would be proud of. So in a sense it is, yet it is the differences between what is happening today and what happened when St Pancras was first built that are most conspicuous. In railway building as in every other endeavour, history never quite repeats itself.

The works carried out today and those promoted by the Midland Railway in the 1860s have in common that they both started with an Act of Parliament. Thereafter the differences soon reveal themselves. For a start, Barlow and Scott were confident of having a cleared site and except for the limits set by neighbouring landowners and uses, they had a generally free hand. By contrast, today's project has been conceived of as a way of reusing what already exists rather than starting afresh. It knits together and extends the infrastructure that is already available: indeed it could never have been dreamt of if there was not a legacy of existing railways, underground and roads to depend on.

As well as being functionally reliant on what already exists, today's project is also far more historically self-conscious. No-one was more historically-minded than Scott, but the past he drew upon was unfettered and wide ranging. It certainly had nothing to do with the immediate context of the site where the station was built. But now it is his building, hugely admired and listed Grade 1, which helps form the context to which the new works defer. Every step in the design of the station extension has been tested for how it will relate to Barlow and Scott's achievement, a relationship treated as being just as important as the functional necessities of the project.

Another issue which has helped shape the new works is an inherited suspicion of the impact of any new development, something felt far more strongly now than in the 1860s. So what is now being built, or is proposed, is circumscribed by regulations and requirements that would have astonished James Allport and the Midland directors. The justification for the railway project, prepared for the enabling Bill, runs to countless volumes and although the idea of a Heritage Deed of Agreement was intended to simplify the administration of the conservation aspects of the works it has in fact resulted in just as many negotiations and exchanges of paper. Likewise, the process required to justify bringing the hotel back into use has been enough to try the patience of a Job. The result is that today's project is far more cautious than its predecessor.

But ultimately what distinguishes today's developments is not just the procedures involved but the end result. St Pancras has some claim to a place in the history of international train services because of its modest role as a terminus for boat trains from Tilbury. However that obscure aspect of its history in no way anticipates the role it has now been called on to play. When it opens as an international terminus and receives its first trains from France and Belgium it will decisively regain the prominence which it had when first built. In fact it will have achieved what the Midland directors always intended, a reputation of being in a class of its own.

[1] J Betjeman, *London's Historic Railway Stations* (1972), 15.

[2] *The Victorian Society Annual Report* 1967-8, 11-13. Notes of the Buckingham Palace meeting, 27th February 1968 in the Jack Simmons papers (I am grateful to Professor J. Mordaunt Crook for showing me the relevant file).

[3] *Times*, 24 December 1968, 1.

[4] Bernard Kaukas, 'St Pancras Revisited', *London Journal* 8 (Winter 1982), 191-203.

[5] T D Stevenson, 'Electrification of the Midland Suburban Railway Line from London to Bedford: Civil Engineering Aspects', *Proceedings of the Institution of Civil Engineers* 82 Part 1 (August 1987), 735-53. The inauguration of the BedPan service was delayed because of a dispute over the introduction of driver-only operation.

[6] Brian Perren, 'Thameslink', *Modern Railways*, 45 (April 1988), 201-8.

[7] Robert Thorne *et al*, 'King's Cross Goods Yard', in Michael Hunter and Robert Thorne, *Change at King's Cross* (1990), 91-109.

[8] Michael Hunter, 'King's Cross: History in the Making', in Hunter and Thorne *op.cit.*, 128-29.

[9] King's Cross Railway Lands Group, *King's Cross Project. Costs and Financial Viability* (May 1992), 4,20.

[10] *Evening Standard*, 10 October 1991, 7,13; *Rail*, 30 October 1991, 34-35.

[11] *New Civil Engineer*, 31 October 1991, 5; *Architects' Journal*, 13 November 1991, 24-27.

[12] *Independent*, 23 December 1992, 2.

[13] *Observer*, 28 March 1993. On Liverpool Street see Robert Thorne and Christopher Haddon, 'Epic Journey', *Architects' Journal*, 6 May 1992, 24-35.

[14] *Times*, 25 January 1994, 1, 3.

[15] Nick Derbyshire even considered building the whole departure lounge within the end gable of the trainshed.

[16] The Victorian Society, *The CTRL Terminus at St. Pancras: Victorian Society Concerns About the Conservation Regime* (June 1996).

[17] David Loosemore and Neil Shepherd, 'Planning High Speed Railways in Europe: an Update' *Arup Journal* 31 Part 1 (1996), 3-5; *New Civil Engineer*, 29 February 1996, 3. One further complication was that in April 1995 the ownership of Union Railways passed from British Railways to the Department of Transport.

[18] John Gough, 'All change at St Pancras', *Modern Railways* (November 2001), 44-47.

[19] Speyhawk and YRM Partnership Ltd, *The Midland Grand Hotel & St. Pancras Centre* (July 1987); Gavin Stamp, 'Heart Surgery at St Pancras', *Designers' Journal* 36 (April 1988), 52-55.

[20] M Davies, 'Conservation of St Pancras Chambers, Designed as the Midland Grand Hotel', in N S Baer *et al*, *Conservation of Historic Brick Structures* (Shaftesbury, 1998), 393 – 406.

[21] Margaret and Richard Davies, 'St Pancras Chambers London: Conservation of the Wall and Ceiling Paintings in the Grand Stair', *Transactions of the Association for Studies in the conservation of Historic Buildings* 19 (1994), 57-60. The restoration of the vault was carried out by International Fine Art Conservation Studios Limited.

[22] Ken Cordner, 'Ten Months to Go', *Modern Railways* (December 2002), 34-46; 'Underground at King's Cross', *New Civil Engineer* Special Report, 20 February 2003, 1-XV.

Appendix 1

Passenger Traffic and Working Expenses
1872-1922

The table below (compiled from PRO: RAIL 491/672 p293; RAIL 491/674, p306; RAIL 491/675, p325; RAIL 491/676 p352; and RAIL 491/677, p353), shows the growth of traffic at St Pancras station over almost the whole period of the Midland Company's ownership. The figures given in col. 4 include, down to 1901, receipts for the carriage of parcels, horses, carriages, and dogs, as well as of passnegers. From 1902 onwards parcels were accounted for separately, and they are omitted here.

These figures are apparently unique. No comparable series for any other London station seems to exist. For Paddington there are figures for 1903, 1913 and 1923, showing a growth in the number of passengers from 1,706,452 in the first year to 2,394,513 in the last, with a corresponding growth in receipts of £754,302 to £1,647,243 (PRO: *GWR Traffic dealt with at stations and goods depots, 1938*). There are figures for Victoria (Brighton) for each year from 1894 to 1901, the number of passengers starting at 4,114,322 and rising to its peak in the Paris Exhibition year of 1900 with 4,849,176. (PRO: RAIL 414/120: Report of January 8, 1902.)

Year	No. of passengers booked	No. of season tickets	Total coaching receipts	Working expenses of station
1872	170,925	---	96,537	9,647
1873	187,897	---	98,600	8,628
1874	206,210	---	108,892	9,459
1875	242,227	---	129,868	10,254
1876	272,375	---	167,538	11,114
1877	289,899	---	190,628	14,176
1878	311,256	---	202,213	15,191
1879	317,767	---	198,783	15,184
1880	334,255	---	215,856	16,750
1881	353,893	---	285,077	17,823
1882	377,126	---	244,658	19,431
1883	405,562	---	249,509	19,625
1884	403,585	528	256,585	20,387

APPENDIX 1

Year	No. of passengers booked	No. of season tickets	Total coaching receipts	Working expenses of station
1885	402,577	601	256,670	21,374
1886	425,072	645	264,332	21,192
1887	414,565	672	265,619	21,540
1888	419,722	746	269,671	25,047
1889	438,005	806	280,903	24,010
1890	442,816	875	286,996	24,891
1891	452,929	811	296,952	26,874
1892	461,761	888	289,628	25,687
1893	468,005	978	295,657	26,041
1894	492,876	1,192	303,834	26,116
1895	505,775	1,119	313,195	25,869
1896	559,788	1,457	549,488	26,860
1897	596,482	1,747	370,154	28,967
1898	626,782	1,653	371,212	30,736
1899	633,393	1,875	377,503	31,608
1900	652,378	2,028	386,578	33,975
1901	701,807	2,208	421,391	36,458
1902	730,749	2,155	371,963	26,124
1903	815,762	2,440	395,810	24,745
1904	832,812	2,573	405,335	26,128
1905	841,601	2,613	400,677	25,165
1906	853,082	2,765	425,891	24,883
1907	863,586	2,937	431,554	24,846
1908	830,730	2,903	431,174	23,660
1909	812,681	2,872	413,657	22,203
1910	829,058	2,999	457,290	21,396
1911	857,117	2,748	442,347	21,728
1912	851,934	2,656	449,977	22,819
1913	882,253	2,595	458,660	23,820
1914	886,570	2,537	436,505	22,975
1915	923,463	2,159	436,819	21,776
1916	977,247	2,097	484,755	21,846
1917	774,447	3,094	553,647	24,567
1918	899,258	2,491	611,625	33,992
1919	1,138,905	2,355	756,418	48,984
1920	1,188,629	2,612	887,155	64,878
1921	1,029,786	2,571	866,936	63,667
1922	1,028,010	2,534	872,599	54,781

Appendix 2

Scott's Drawings

The Midland Company was proud of its set of Scott's plans and drawings. The St. Pancras Hotel Committee resolved in 1881 that they were "to be kept in their original state, no alteration whatever to be made to them" (PRO: RAIL 491/275, min. 52). Unfortunately only a small number of these survive today, and none of them show the hotel as finally built.

The drawings which have survived are in two collections:

> The RIBA Drawings Collection, where they are listed as group 89 in the collection of Scott drawings. These were given to the RIBA by Scott's descendants.
> The Public Record Office, listed as part of the Midland Railway archive (RAIL 491). These presumably came to the PRO from British Railways.

Each collection includes drawings from two stages in the evolution of the design:

> The original competition design:
> RIBA 89, 1-19 and PRO RAIL 491/580-1. Of this stage the RIBA drawings include T.G. Jackson's perspective of the Coffee Room (see Plate xx).

> The reduced, five storey scheme as approved in 1866: RIBA 89, 20-34 and PRO RAIL 491/1164-86.

Some of Scott's drawings were engraved for publication in the building press, notably *The Engineer*, May 31st 1867 and June 14th 1867.